Fueling the Future Understanding Biofuel Policies and Regulations

Astrid

Copyright © [2023]

Title: Fueling the Future Understanding Biofuel Policies and Regulations

Author's: Astrid.

All rights reserved. No part of this publication may be reproduced, stored in a retrieval system, or transmitted in any form or by any means, electronic, mechanical, photocopying, recording, or otherwise, without the prior written permission of the publisher or author, except in the case of brief quotations embodied in critical reviews and certain other non-commercial uses permitted by copyright law.

This book was printed and published by [Publisher's: Astrid] in [2023]

ISBN:

TABLE OF CONTENTS

Chapter 1: Introduction to Biofuel Policies and Regulations 07

Definition and Importance of Biofuels

Overview of Global Biofuel Industry

The Need for Biofuel Policies and Regulations

Objectives of the Book

Chapter 2: Historical Development of Biofuel Policies 15

Early Biofuel Initiatives

Evolution of Biofuel Policies and Regulations

Case Studies: Successful Biofuel Policy Implementation

Chapter 3: Types of Biofuels and their Production Processes 22

First Generation Biofuels: Ethanol and Biodiesel

Second Generation Biofuels: Cellulosic Ethanol and Algae-based Biofuels

Third Generation Biofuels: Synthetic Biofuels

Comparison of Biofuel Production Processes

Chapter 4: International Biofuel Policies and Regulations 30

United States Biofuel Policies and Regulations

Renewable Fuel Standard (RFS)

Biofuel Tax Incentives

European Union Biofuel Policies and Regulations

Renewable Energy Directive (RED)

Sustainability Criteria for Biofuels

Biofuel Policies in Developing Countries

Brazil

Indonesia

India

Chapter 5: Environmental and Social Impacts of Biofuels 50

Greenhouse Gas Emissions Reduction Potential

Land Use Change and Deforestation

Water Consumption and Pollution

Food Security and Agricultural Practices

Social and Economic Implications

Chapter 6: Challenges and Opportunities in Biofuel Policy Implementation 61

Technological and Infrastructural Challenges

Economic Considerations and Market Dynamics

Stakeholder Engagement and Public Perception

Future Opportunities and Potential Solutions

Chapter 7: Case Studies on Biofuel Policies and Regulations 69

Case Study 1: United States' Renewable Fuel Standard

Case Study 2: European Union's Renewable Energy Directive

Case Study 3: Brazil's Ethanol Program

Case Study 4: Indonesia's Palm Oil-based Biofuel Initiative

Chapter 8: Evaluating the Effectiveness of Biofuel Policies and Regulations 79

Metrics for Assessing Policy Impact

Comparative Analysis of Biofuel Policies

Lessons Learned and Best Practices

Recommendations for Future Policy Development

Chapter 9: The Future of Biofuel Policies and Regulations 87

Emerging Technologies and Biofuel Alternatives

Shifting Paradigms in Policy Approaches

Global Collaboration and Harmonization Efforts

Sustainable Biofuel Pathways for a Greener Future

Chapter 10: Conclusion 95

Summary of Key Findings

Implications for Biofuel Industry and Stakeholders

Call to Action: Moving Towards a Sustainable Biofuel Future

Chapter 1: Introduction to Biofuel Policies and Regulations

Definition and Importance of Biofuels

Biofuels are a type of renewable energy derived from organic materials, including plants, algae, and animal waste. They are considered an essential alternative to fossil fuels due to their lower carbon emissions and potential for reducing greenhouse gases. In recent years, biofuels have gained significant attention as a sustainable energy source, offering a viable solution to the global energy crisis and addressing environmental concerns.

The importance of biofuels lies in their potential to reduce dependence on fossil fuels, which are finite resources and major contributors to climate change. Unlike traditional fuels, biofuels can be produced from a wide range of organic materials, making them more versatile and accessible. By harnessing the power of nature, biofuels offer a sustainable option for meeting the growing energy demands of the world.

One of the primary benefits of biofuels is their ability to reduce greenhouse gas emissions. When burned, biofuels release carbon dioxide (CO_2) into the atmosphere, but they absorb an equal amount of CO_2 during their growth, resulting in a carbon-neutral cycle. This is in contrast to fossil fuels, which release large amounts of CO_2 that have been sequestered for millions of years, leading to a net increase in greenhouse gases.

Additionally, biofuels play a crucial role in mitigating air pollution and promoting cleaner air quality. They produce significantly lower levels of harmful pollutants, such as sulfur oxides and particulate matter, which are major contributors to respiratory diseases and environmental degradation. By adopting biofuels as an alternative to conventional fuels, we can improve the air quality in urban areas and reduce the health risks associated with pollution.

Biofuels also offer economic benefits by promoting rural development and creating new job opportunities. The production of biofuels often involves agricultural activities, which can stimulate economic growth in rural areas and provide a sustainable income for farmers. Furthermore, investing in biofuel technologies and infrastructure can drive innovation and create a green economy, fostering a transition towards a more sustainable future.

In conclusion, biofuels are a vital component of the world's energy mix, offering a renewable and environmentally friendly alternative to fossil fuels. With their ability to reduce greenhouse gas emissions, mitigate air pollution, and contribute to economic development, biofuels have the potential to shape a more sustainable and prosperous future for all. By understanding the definition and importance of biofuels, we can actively participate in the transition towards a cleaner and greener world.

Overview of Global Biofuel Industry

The global biofuel industry has emerged as a promising solution to meet the growing energy demands of the world while reducing reliance on fossil fuels and mitigating climate change. This subchapter provides an overview of the global biofuel industry, highlighting its significance, key players, and future prospects.

Biofuels, derived from renewable organic sources such as crops, waste materials, and algae, offer a sustainable alternative to traditional fossil fuels. They are primarily used in transportation, replacing or blending with gasoline and diesel fuels. The biofuel industry plays a crucial role in promoting energy security, reducing greenhouse gas emissions, and fostering rural development.

The global biofuel market has witnessed significant growth over the past decade. Several countries, including the United States, Brazil, Germany, and China, have implemented supportive policies and regulations to promote biofuel production and consumption. These policies include mandates, tax incentives, and subsidies, which have encouraged investment in research and development, infrastructure, and production capacity.

The key players in the global biofuel industry include biofuel producers, feedstock suppliers, technology providers, and government organizations. Major biofuel producers such as Archer Daniels Midland (ADM), Poet, and Neste Oil have invested heavily in expanding their production capacity and developing advanced biofuel technologies. Feedstock suppliers, such as corn, sugarcane, soybean, and palm oil producers, play a crucial role in ensuring a sustainable and reliable supply of raw materials.

The future prospects of the global biofuel industry are promising. The increasing global demand for energy, coupled with concerns over climate change and the depletion of fossil fuel reserves, has led to a growing interest in biofuels. Technological advancements, such as the development of second-generation biofuels from non-food feedstocks and the utilization of waste materials, are expected to further enhance the efficiency and sustainability of biofuel production.

However, the biofuel industry also faces challenges. The competition for land and water resources, potential environmental impacts, and concerns over food security are among the key issues that need to be addressed. Additionally, the volatility of fossil fuel prices and the uncertain regulatory environment pose risks to biofuel investments.

In conclusion, the global biofuel industry represents a significant opportunity to address energy and environmental challenges. With supportive policies, technological innovations, and sustainable practices, biofuels have the potential to revolutionize the global energy landscape. However, careful consideration of the social, economic, and environmental implications is essential to ensure the long-term viability and success of the biofuel industry.

The Need for Biofuel Policies and Regulations

In recent years, the world has witnessed a growing interest in alternative energy sources, particularly biofuels, as a means to reduce reliance on fossil fuels and combat climate change. Biofuels, derived from organic matter such as crops, agricultural residues, and even algae, offer a promising solution to the energy crisis and environmental challenges we face today. However, to fully harness the potential of biofuels and ensure their sustainable development, it is essential to have comprehensive biofuel policies and regulations in place.

One of the primary reasons for the need of biofuel policies and regulations is to address the environmental concerns associated with fossil fuel consumption. The burning of fossil fuels releases greenhouse gases into the atmosphere, contributing to global warming and climate change. Biofuels, on the other hand, are considered carbon-neutral as the carbon dioxide emitted during their combustion is offset by the carbon dioxide absorbed by the plants during their growth. By implementing biofuel policies and regulations, governments can encourage the use of biofuels as a greener alternative to fossil fuels and reduce carbon emissions.

Moreover, biofuel policies and regulations can also help promote energy security and reduce dependence on imported fossil fuels. Many countries heavily rely on oil imports, which not only puts a strain on their economies but also leaves them vulnerable to geopolitical tensions and price fluctuations. By supporting the development and production of biofuels, governments can enhance energy independence and diversify their energy sources, thereby increasing energy security.

Furthermore, biofuel policies and regulations can stimulate economic growth and create new job opportunities. The biofuel industry has the potential to generate significant economic benefits, from farming and harvesting biofuel feedstocks to manufacturing and distributing biofuels. By providing incentives and support for the biofuel sector, governments can foster innovation, attract investments, and create a sustainable green economy.

However, without proper policies and regulations, the biofuel industry may face challenges related to sustainability, land use, and food security. For instance, large-scale cultivation of biofuel crops can lead to deforestation, habitat destruction, and competition with food production. By implementing regulations that promote sustainable practices, protect biodiversity, and ensure responsible land use, governments can mitigate these potential adverse impacts and ensure that biofuel production is environmentally and socially responsible.

In conclusion, the need for biofuel policies and regulations cannot be overstated. By establishing a clear framework for the development, production, and use of biofuels, governments can promote sustainable energy practices, reduce greenhouse gas emissions, enhance energy security, and stimulate economic growth. The successful implementation of such policies and regulations will pave the way for a future powered by clean, renewable, and environmentally-friendly biofuels.

Objectives of the Book

Welcome to "Fueling the Future: Understanding Biofuel Policies and Regulations." In this subchapter, we will delve into the objectives of this book and provide an overview of what you can expect to gain from reading it. Whether you are a biofuel enthusiast, a policy-maker, an industry professional, or simply someone interested in sustainable energy solutions, this book aims to offer valuable insights into the world of biofuels.

The primary objective of this book is to provide a comprehensive understanding of biofuel policies and regulations. Biofuels have gained significant attention in recent years as a potential solution to mitigate climate change and reduce reliance on fossil fuels. However, navigating the complex landscape of biofuel policies and regulations can be challenging for both experts and newcomers to the field. This book aims to bridge that gap by offering a clear and concise overview of the key policies and regulations governing the biofuel industry.

By reading this book, you will gain a deep understanding of the different types of biofuels, their production processes, and their environmental and economic impacts. We will explore the various policies and regulations implemented by governments around the world to promote the development and use of biofuels. From renewable fuel standards to tax incentives, we will examine how these policies shape the biofuel market and influence its growth.

Furthermore, this book aims to provide a balanced perspective on biofuel policies and their implications. We will discuss the benefits and challenges associated with biofuel production and address key debates surrounding issues such as land use, food security, and greenhouse gas emissions. By presenting diverse viewpoints and scientific evidence, we hope to foster informed discussions and empower readers to form their own opinions on biofuel policies.

In addition to policy analysis, this book will also highlight success stories and best practices from around the world. We will showcase examples of countries and regions that have effectively implemented biofuel policies, leading to significant reductions in carbon emissions and enhanced energy security. By learning from these experiences, readers will gain valuable insights into how biofuel policies can be effectively designed and implemented.

In conclusion, "Fueling the Future: Understanding Biofuel Policies and Regulations" aims to be a valuable resource for anyone interested in the world of biofuels. Whether you are an industry professional, a policy-maker, or simply a curious individual, this book will equip you with the knowledge and understanding needed to navigate the complex world of biofuel policies and contribute to a more sustainable future.

Chapter 2: Historical Development of Biofuel Policies

Early Biofuel Initiatives

Biofuels, also known as renewable fuels, have gained significant attention in recent years due to their potential to reduce greenhouse gas emissions and dependence on fossil fuels. However, the concept of biofuels is not new; early biofuel initiatives date back several decades. In this subchapter, we will explore the beginnings of biofuel development, highlighting important milestones and initiatives that laid the foundation for the biofuel industry we see today.

The history of biofuels can be traced back to the 19th century when Rudolf Diesel, the inventor of the diesel engine, envisioned that his engine could run on vegetable oils. This vision laid the groundwork for the development of vegetable oil-based fuels, which are now known as biodiesel. Although Diesel's idea was not immediately implemented due to the low availability of vegetable oils at that time, it planted the seed for future biofuel innovations.

Fast forward to the 20th century, the oil crisis of the 1970s sparked renewed interest in biofuels. As concerns over energy security and rising oil prices grew, governments and researchers began exploring alternative fuel options. The United States, for example, launched the Biomass Energy Program in the 1970s, which aimed to develop biofuels from agricultural residues and dedicated energy crops.

Another significant milestone in early biofuel initiatives was the establishment of the Brazilian ethanol program in the 1970s. Facing difficulties in meeting its oil demand, Brazil turned to sugarcane as a feedstock for ethanol production. The successful implementation of the ethanol program not only reduced Brazil's dependence on imported oil but also provided economic opportunities for rural communities and contributed to a significant reduction in carbon emissions.

In the 1990s, the European Union (EU) recognized the potential of biofuels and began implementing policies to promote their use. The EU's biofuel initiatives were primarily driven by environmental concerns, aiming to reduce greenhouse gas emissions and combat climate change. These early efforts laid the foundation for the EU's Renewable Energy Directive, which set binding targets for the use of renewable energy, including biofuels, within the member states.

The early biofuel initiatives highlighted in this subchapter demonstrate the long-standing interest and commitment to developing sustainable energy sources. These initiatives paved the way for further research and development, leading to the diverse range of biofuels available today. Understanding these early milestones is crucial for appreciating the progress made in biofuel policies and regulations and provides context for the challenges and opportunities faced by the biofuel industry as it continues to evolve and shape our energy future.

In conclusion, early biofuel initiatives have played a vital role in the development and growth of the biofuel industry. From Rudolf Diesel's vision to the establishment of national programs and policies, these initiatives have set the stage for the widespread adoption of biofuels as a renewable energy source. As we move forward, it is essential to build upon the successes and lessons learned from these early initiatives to further refine and expand the use of biofuels, ensuring a sustainable and cleaner future for all.

Evolution of Biofuel Policies and Regulations

Biofuels have emerged as a promising alternative to traditional fossil fuels, offering a renewable and sustainable solution to meet the world's growing energy demands while reducing greenhouse gas emissions. However, the journey towards the widespread adoption of biofuels has been shaped by a multitude of policies and regulations that have evolved over the years.

This subchapter explores the fascinating evolution of biofuel policies and regulations, shedding light on their importance in shaping the biofuel industry and driving its growth. By understanding the historical context and the rationale behind these policies, individuals in the biofuel niche and beyond can better comprehend the challenges, opportunities, and potential future developments in this field.

The journey of biofuel policies can be traced back to the energy crises of the 1970s when countries sought to reduce their dependence on imported oil. This led to the introduction of blending mandates, which required a certain percentage of biofuels to be mixed with conventional fuels. These mandates aimed to promote domestic biofuel production, diversify energy sources, and enhance energy security.

As concerns about climate change and environmental degradation grew, governments worldwide began implementing more comprehensive policies and regulations to promote sustainable biofuel production. These initiatives focused on minimizing the environmental impact of biofuel production, ensuring land use sustainability, and preventing deforestation. They also aimed to encourage research and development in advanced biofuel technologies, such as cellulosic ethanol and algae-based biodiesel.

Over time, biofuel policies and regulations have become more sophisticated, taking into account social, economic, and environmental factors. Governments have introduced certification schemes, sustainability criteria, and lifecycle analysis to evaluate the overall sustainability and carbon intensity of biofuels. These developments have helped to address concerns regarding indirect land use change, water usage, and food security associated with biofuel production.

Furthermore, international collaborations and agreements have played a significant role in harmonizing biofuel policies and ensuring a level playing field for biofuel producers across different countries. Organizations like the International Energy Agency (IEA), the United Nations Framework Convention on Climate Change (UNFCCC), and the European Union (EU) have been instrumental in facilitating global cooperation and knowledge-sharing in biofuel policy development.

As the world continues to grapple with the challenges of climate change and transitioning to a low-carbon economy, biofuel policies and regulations will continue to evolve. The subchapter concludes by highlighting the potential future directions in biofuel policy, including the integration of biofuels into broader renewable energy frameworks, the promotion of advanced biofuel technologies, and the exploration of novel feedstocks and production methods.

By delving into the evolution of biofuel policies and regulations, this subchapter aims to provide a comprehensive understanding of the historical context, current state, and future outlook of the biofuel industry. Whether you are an industry professional, a policy-maker, or simply an interested individual, this knowledge is essential for navigating the dynamic landscape of biofuel policies and regulations and contributing to a sustainable and greener future.

Case Studies: Successful Biofuel Policy Implementation

In today's world, where the need for sustainable energy sources is increasing exponentially, biofuels have emerged as a viable alternative to traditional fossil fuels. As governments and industries strive to reduce greenhouse gas emissions and promote renewable energy, successful biofuel policy implementation plays a crucial role in achieving these goals. This subchapter explores some noteworthy case studies that illuminate the effectiveness of biofuel policies in various countries across the globe.

One such case study involves Brazil, a leading player in the biofuel industry. Brazil's success story stems from its long-standing commitment to biofuels, particularly ethanol derived from sugarcane. The Brazilian government implemented a series of policies that encouraged the production and consumption of ethanol, including tax incentives, mandatory blending requirements, and investment in research and development. As a result, Brazil now boasts a transportation sector that heavily relies on renewable biofuels, significantly reducing its dependence on imported fossil fuels.

Moving to Europe, we find another remarkable case study in the form of Sweden. Sweden's biofuel policy implementation has been driven by a strong commitment to achieving carbon neutrality. The government introduced generous financial incentives for the production and use of biofuels, including tax exemptions and grants. Additionally, Sweden implemented a comprehensive certification system, ensuring that biofuels meet strict sustainability criteria. These efforts have led to a substantial increase in the use of biofuels, particularly in the transportation and heating sectors, contributing to Sweden's ambitious climate targets.

In the United States, the Renewable Fuel Standard (RFS) has been instrumental in promoting biofuel production and consumption. The RFS mandates the blending of renewable fuels, such as ethanol and biodiesel, into transportation fuels. This policy has not only reduced greenhouse gas emissions but also stimulated rural economies by creating new markets for agricultural products. The RFS has proven to be a successful model for biofuel policy implementation, although challenges such as infrastructure limitations and conflicting interests continue to be addressed.

These case studies highlight the importance of well-designed and effectively implemented biofuel policies. By providing financial incentives, establishing blending requirements, promoting research and development, and ensuring sustainability, governments can catalyze the growth of the biofuel industry. Moreover, successful biofuel policy implementation not only contributes to reducing carbon emissions and enhancing energy security but also fosters economic development and the creation of green jobs.

In conclusion, the case studies presented in this subchapter demonstrate the positive outcomes of successful biofuel policy implementation. Brazil, Sweden, and the United States serve as inspirations for other countries looking to adopt similar strategies. By learning from these experiences and tailoring policies to fit their specific contexts, governments can accelerate the transition towards a sustainable and renewable energy future.

Chapter 3: Types of Biofuels and their Production Processes

First Generation Biofuels: Ethanol and Biodiesel

As we navigate the ever-increasing demand for energy and the urgency to find sustainable alternatives, biofuels have emerged as a promising solution. Biofuels, derived from renewable organic materials such as plants and agricultural waste, offer a cleaner and more environmentally friendly option compared to traditional fossil fuels. In this subchapter, we delve into the world of first-generation biofuels, specifically ethanol and biodiesel, which have played a pivotal role in shaping the biofuel industry.

Ethanol, often produced from corn, sugarcane, or other high-starch crops, is the most widely used biofuel globally. It is primarily used as a transportation fuel and is blended with gasoline to reduce greenhouse gas emissions. Ethanol's popularity stems from its ability to replace a significant portion of traditional gasoline without requiring extensive modifications to existing vehicles or infrastructure. Additionally, its production is relatively less complex compared to other biofuels, making it cost-effective and readily available.

Biodiesel, on the other hand, is derived from vegetable oils, animal fats, or recycled cooking oils. It serves as a direct substitute for diesel fuel and offers similar energy content and combustion characteristics. Biodiesel reduces emissions of harmful pollutants such as sulfur and particulate matter, making it an attractive alternative for diesel-powered vehicles. Moreover, its production can utilize waste materials, thereby reducing waste disposal problems and promoting a circular economy.

While ethanol and biodiesel have shown immense potential, they are not without limitations. One major concern is the impact on food prices and land use. The use of food crops, such as corn and sugarcane, for biofuel production can lead to increased competition for resources and potential food shortages. Furthermore, the expansion of agricultural land for biofuel crops can contribute to deforestation and habitat destruction. These challenges have prompted researchers to explore alternative feedstocks, including non-food crops and agricultural waste, to mitigate these concerns.

In recent years, the focus of biofuel development has shifted towards second and third-generation biofuels, which offer greater sustainability and reduced environmental impact. However, first-generation biofuels like ethanol and biodiesel continue to play a significant role in the transition towards a more sustainable energy future.

Understanding the complexities and implications of biofuel policies and regulations is crucial for policymakers, researchers, and the general public alike. By delving into the world of first-generation biofuels, we gain valuable insights into their advantages, limitations, and the need for sustainable alternatives. As we strive to fuel the future, it is essential to strike a balance between the demand for energy, environmental considerations, and social implications. Biofuels, including ethanol and biodiesel, remain key players in this transformative journey towards a greener and more sustainable world.

Second Generation Biofuels: Cellulosic Ethanol and Algae-based Biofuels

With the increasing concerns about climate change and the need for sustainable energy sources, biofuels have emerged as a promising alternative to fossil fuels. While first-generation biofuels, such as corn ethanol and soybean biodiesel, have paved the way for the industry, their limitations have led to the development of second-generation biofuels.

This subchapter explores two significant types of second-generation biofuels: cellulosic ethanol and algae-based biofuels. These advanced biofuels offer numerous advantages over their predecessors, including higher energy yields, lower greenhouse gas emissions, and reduced competition with food production.

Cellulosic ethanol is derived from plant matter, such as agricultural residues, grasses, or wood chips, that contain cellulose and hemicellulose. Unlike first-generation biofuels, which use the starch and oil content of crops, cellulosic ethanol production utilizes the entire plant biomass. This makes it a more sustainable and efficient option, as it maximizes the energy potential of the feedstocks. Moreover, since cellulosic ethanol can be produced from non-food crops and waste materials, it does not compete with food production, which has been a major concern with first-generation biofuels.

Algae-based biofuels, on the other hand, offer even greater potential as a sustainable and renewable energy source. Algae, a diverse group of photosynthetic organisms, can produce oils that can be converted into biodiesel. Algae have a much higher lipid content than traditional crops, making them more efficient in terms of energy output per unit of land. Additionally, algae can be cultivated in various environments, including wastewater, reducing the need for freshwater resources.

Both cellulosic ethanol and algae-based biofuels have faced technological and economic challenges in their commercialization. However, recent advancements in biotechnology and process optimization are bringing these biofuels closer to viability. Various research and development initiatives, as well as government support, are catalyzing the growth of these industries.

As the world seeks to transition to a low-carbon future, second-generation biofuels hold great promise. These advanced biofuels not only offer a sustainable alternative to fossil fuels but also have the potential to rejuvenate rural economies by creating new opportunities for farmers and biofuel producers. By understanding the advancements and challenges in cellulosic ethanol and algae-based biofuels, we can contribute to the development and adoption of these innovative solutions for a cleaner and more sustainable energy future.

In conclusion, second-generation biofuels, such as cellulosic ethanol and algae-based biofuels, offer a more sustainable and efficient alternative to traditional fossil fuels. These advanced biofuels have the potential to address the limitations of first-generation biofuels, such as competition with food production and lower energy yields. With ongoing research and development efforts, second-generation biofuels are poised to play a significant role in fueling the future and reducing our dependence on finite fossil fuel resources.

Third Generation Biofuels: Synthetic Biofuels

In recent years, the global effort to reduce greenhouse gas emissions and combat climate change has led to the exploration of alternative energy sources. Biofuels, derived from renewable biological materials, have emerged as a promising solution to meet our energy demands while reducing our reliance on fossil fuels. While first and second-generation biofuels have made significant strides, the third generation of biofuels, known as synthetic biofuels, offers even greater potential for a sustainable future.

Synthetic biofuels are produced through a process called synthetic biology, which involves the manipulation of genetic materials to create new organisms capable of producing biofuels. Unlike traditional biofuels that rely on food crops such as corn or sugarcane, synthetic biofuels can be derived from a wide range of feedstocks, including agricultural waste, algae, and even carbon dioxide emissions. This versatility not only helps to avoid competition between biofuel production and food production but also mitigates the environmental impact associated with land-use change.

One of the key advantages of synthetic biofuels is their remarkable energy density. These fuels have a higher energy content compared to traditional biofuels, making them more efficient and capable of delivering greater power. Additionally, synthetic biofuels have a lower carbon footprint, as they can be tailored to produce fuels with reduced emissions of greenhouse gases. This aspect is crucial in achieving our climate goals and transitioning to a low-carbon economy.

Moreover, synthetic biofuels offer an opportunity to utilize waste materials that would otherwise be discarded, reducing the burden on landfills and promoting a circular economy. By converting waste into valuable energy sources, we can simultaneously address waste management issues and contribute to a more sustainable energy system.

However, the development and commercialization of synthetic biofuels face various challenges. High production costs, technical complexities, and regulatory barriers are some of the obstacles that need to be overcome. Nevertheless, governments, research institutions, and private enterprises are investing in research and development to advance this promising technology.

As we strive to fuel the future sustainably, synthetic biofuels are poised to play a significant role in our energy transition. Their potential to reduce greenhouse gas emissions, promote waste utilization, and enhance energy efficiency makes them a compelling option for a wide range of applications, including transportation, power generation, and industrial processes. With continued innovation and supportive policies, synthetic biofuels can pave the way for a greener and more resilient future.

Whether you are an individual interested in sustainable energy solutions or a professional in the biofuel industry, understanding the potential of synthetic biofuels is essential. By embracing this third generation of biofuels, we can collectively work towards a cleaner and more sustainable future for all.

Comparison of Biofuel Production Processes

Biofuels have emerged as a viable alternative to traditional fossil fuels, offering a promising solution to the environmental concerns associated with greenhouse gas emissions and finite oil reserves. As the demand for renewable energy sources continues to grow, it is crucial to understand the different biofuel production processes and their implications. This subchapter aims to provide an overview and comparison of various biofuel production methods.

1. First-generation Biofuels: First-generation biofuels, also known as conventional biofuels, are produced from agricultural crops such as corn, sugarcane, and vegetable oils. These crops undergo a process called fermentation, where their sugars are converted into ethanol or biodiesel. While first-generation biofuels have been widely adopted due to their ease of production and compatibility with existing engines, they have faced criticism for their impact on food security and land use.

2. Second-generation Biofuels: Second-generation biofuels are derived from non-food feedstocks, including agricultural and forestry residues, algae, and dedicated energy crops. These feedstocks undergo a more complex process called cellulosic conversion, where their lignocellulosic components are broken down into fermentable sugars and subsequently converted into biofuels. Second-generation biofuels offer several advantages over their first-generation counterparts, including a reduced impact on food production and increased potential for carbon sequestration.

3. Third-generation Biofuels: Third-generation biofuels primarily focus on the production of algae-based biofuels. Algae can be cultivated in various environments,

including ponds, bioreactors, and even wastewater, making them highly versatile and scalable. Algae-based biofuels have the potential to yield higher energy outputs and do not compete with food crops for land or freshwater resources. However, the production process, including algae cultivation and oil extraction, still requires optimization to achieve cost-effectiveness on a commercial scale.

4. Fourth-generation Biofuels: Fourth-generation biofuels are a relatively new concept that aims to integrate biofuel production with other industrial processes, such as waste management and carbon capture. These biofuels are designed to be produced using waste materials or CO_2 captured from industrial emissions. By utilizing waste streams or carbon dioxide, fourth-generation biofuels have the potential to minimize environmental impact and contribute to a circular economy.

In conclusion, biofuel production processes have evolved significantly, offering a range of options that address the limitations of earlier generations while maintaining a focus on sustainability. As the world transitions towards a greener future, understanding the advantages and disadvantages of each biofuel production process is essential for policymakers, researchers, and individuals interested in the biofuel industry. By comparing these processes, we can identify the most efficient and environmentally friendly ways to produce biofuels and accelerate the transition to a more sustainable energy future.

Chapter 4: International Biofuel Policies and Regulations

United States Biofuel Policies and Regulations

In recent years, the United States has been actively working towards reducing its dependence on fossil fuels and promoting the use of renewable energy sources. As a result, biofuels have emerged as a viable alternative to traditional fuels, with the potential to significantly contribute to a more sustainable future. This subchapter aims to provide a comprehensive overview of the biofuel policies and regulations in the United States, highlighting the government's efforts to promote and regulate the biofuel industry.

The United States government has implemented various policies and regulations to support the development and production of biofuels. One of the key initiatives is the Renewable Fuel Standard (RFS), which was established in 2005 and later expanded in 2007. Under the RFS, the Environmental Protection Agency (EPA) sets annual targets for the amount of renewable fuels, including biofuels, that must be blended into the nation's transportation fuel supply. This policy has not only stimulated investment in biofuel production but also created a market for biofuel producers to sell their products.

To further encourage the adoption of biofuels, the government has also introduced tax incentives and grants for biofuel producers and consumers. These incentives aim to reduce the cost of producing biofuels and make them more competitive with traditional fuels. Additionally, the government has invested in research and development programs to improve the efficiency and sustainability of biofuels, with a focus on advanced biofuels derived from non-food feedstocks.

While the United States has made significant progress in promoting biofuels, there are also regulatory challenges that need to be addressed. One such challenge is the potential impact of biofuel production on food prices and land use. The government has implemented sustainability criteria to ensure that biofuels are produced in an environmentally and socially responsible manner, without negatively affecting food security or causing deforestation.

Furthermore, the United States has been actively engaged in international discussions on biofuel policies and regulations. Through collaboration with other countries, the aim is to develop a global framework that promotes sustainable biofuel production and trade.

In conclusion, the United States has taken significant steps to promote the use of biofuels as a renewable energy source. Through policies such as the Renewable Fuel Standard and various incentives, the government has created a favorable environment for the growth of the biofuel industry. However, challenges such as sustainability and international coordination remain, which require ongoing efforts and collaboration to ensure the long-term success of biofuels in the United States and beyond.

Renewable Fuel Standard (RFS)

The Renewable Fuel Standard (RFS) is a significant policy tool implemented by governments worldwide to promote the use of biofuels as an alternative to traditional fossil fuels. This subchapter aims to provide a comprehensive understanding of the RFS, its importance, and the impact it has on the biofuel industry.

The RFS sets specific targets for the blending and consumption of biofuels within a given country or region. These targets are typically implemented through legislation, which mandates that fuel producers and importers meet a certain percentage of their total fuel sales with renewable fuels. By doing so, the RFS encourages the production and use of biofuels, reducing greenhouse gas emissions and dependence on fossil fuels.

One of the main objectives of the RFS is to reduce carbon emissions and mitigate climate change. Biofuels, such as ethanol and biodiesel, are derived from renewable sources like corn, sugarcane, soybeans, and algae. When compared to traditional fossil fuels, these biofuels have lower carbon footprints, contributing to a cleaner environment and a more sustainable future.

The RFS also plays a crucial role in promoting energy security and reducing dependence on imported oil. By diversifying the energy mix and utilizing domestically produced biofuels, countries can enhance their energy independence and reduce vulnerability to oil price fluctuations and supply disruptions.

Additionally, the RFS stimulates economic growth and rural development by creating new markets for agricultural commodities. Biofuel production requires a steady supply of feedstocks, such as crops and waste materials, which provides farmers and rural communities with additional income opportunities. Moreover, the biofuel industry fosters job creation, innovation, and technological advancements, driving economic prosperity.

However, the implementation of the RFS is not without challenges. Critics argue that biofuel production can lead to unintended consequences, such as deforestation, increased food prices, and competition for land and water resources. Balancing the environmental, social, and economic aspects of biofuel production remains a complex task, requiring continuous monitoring, research, and policy adjustments.

In conclusion, the Renewable Fuel Standard (RFS) is a vital policy measure aimed at promoting the use of biofuels as a sustainable and renewable energy source. By setting targets for biofuel consumption, the RFS contributes to reducing carbon emissions, enhancing energy security, and fostering economic growth. However, it is essential to address the challenges associated with biofuel production to ensure a balanced and responsible approach towards achieving a greener and more sustainable future.

Biofuel Tax Incentives

In recent years, there has been a growing global interest in biofuels as a sustainable alternative to traditional fossil fuels. Recognizing the potential of biofuels to reduce greenhouse gas emissions and dependence on non-renewable energy sources, governments around the world have implemented various policies and regulations to incentivize their production and use. One such policy tool is the provision of tax incentives for biofuels.

Tax incentives have proven to be an effective means of promoting the adoption of biofuels by reducing the cost burden for both producers and consumers. These incentives typically take the form of tax credits, exemptions, or reduced tax rates for biofuel producers and distributors. By lowering the costs of production and distribution, these tax incentives make biofuels more economically viable and competitive with conventional fossil fuels.

The primary objective of biofuel tax incentives is to stimulate investment in biofuel production infrastructure and encourage the growth of the biofuel industry. These incentives can include tax breaks for the purchase of equipment and machinery used in biofuel production, as well as tax credits for research and development activities in the field of biofuels. By providing financial support to biofuel producers, governments aim to promote the development of innovative technologies and the expansion of biofuel production capacity.

In addition to promoting the growth of the biofuel industry, tax incentives also aim to incentivize the consumption of biofuels by end-users. This can be achieved through tax credits or exemptions for individuals or businesses that use biofuels in their vehicles or machinery. By reducing the price differential between biofuels and conventional fuels, these incentives encourage consumers to choose biofuels, thus increasing their demand and market share.

It is important to note that the design and implementation of biofuel tax incentives vary across different jurisdictions. Some countries offer comprehensive and long-term tax incentives to support the biofuel industry, while others provide temporary or limited incentives. The effectiveness of these incentives also depends on other factors such as the availability and accessibility of biofuel feedstocks, the presence of a well-developed distribution infrastructure, and the existence of supportive regulatory frameworks.

In conclusion, biofuel tax incentives play a crucial role in promoting the growth and adoption of biofuels. By reducing the financial barriers associated with biofuel production and consumption, these incentives encourage investment, innovation, and market demand for biofuels. However, it is important for policymakers to carefully design and evaluate these incentives to ensure their effectiveness and alignment with broader sustainability goals. As the global demand for clean and renewable energy continues to rise, biofuel tax incentives are likely to remain an important policy tool in the transition towards a more sustainable future.

European Union Biofuel Policies and Regulations

The European Union (EU) has been at the forefront of promoting sustainable energy sources, including biofuels, as part of its commitment to combat climate change and reduce greenhouse gas emissions. In this subchapter, we will delve into the various biofuel policies and regulations implemented by the EU, highlighting their objectives and impacts.

One of the key initiatives introduced by the EU is the Renewable Energy Directive (RED), which sets binding targets for the use of renewable energy in transport. The RED mandates that by 2020, at least 10% of energy consumed in the transport sector should come from renewable sources, including biofuels. This directive has been instrumental in driving the development and adoption of biofuels across member states.

To ensure the sustainability of biofuels, the EU has also established the criteria for biofuels under the RED. These criteria aim to guarantee that biofuels are produced in an environmentally friendly manner, without causing deforestation or other negative impacts on natural habitats. Additionally, the EU has set a minimum greenhouse gas savings threshold for biofuels, ensuring that they offer significant carbon emission reductions compared to fossil fuels.

The EU has also implemented a certification system for biofuels, known as the Renewable Energy Directive II (RED II). This system aims to enhance transparency and traceability of biofuels, providing consumers with information about the sustainability and origin of the biofuels they use. The certification process involves verifying compliance with the sustainability criteria set by the EU, ensuring that biofuels meet the required standards.

Furthermore, the EU has encouraged the development and use of advanced biofuels, which are produced from non-food feedstocks and offer even better environmental performance compared to conventional biofuels. The EU's Advanced Biofuels Initiative supports research, development, and commercialization of advanced biofuels, contributing to the diversification of feedstocks and the reduction of greenhouse gas emissions.

In conclusion, the European Union has adopted a comprehensive set of policies and regulations to promote the use of biofuels as a sustainable energy source. Through initiatives like the Renewable Energy Directive, the EU has set binding targets, sustainability criteria, and certification systems to ensure the environmental viability of biofuels. By encouraging the development of advanced biofuels, the EU is also fostering innovation and driving the transition towards a greener and more sustainable future. These policies and regulations play a crucial role in shaping the biofuel landscape in Europe, contributing to the global efforts to combat climate change and reduce reliance on fossil fuels.

Renewable Energy Directive (RED)

In today's world, where climate change and environmental degradation are becoming increasingly prominent, the need for renewable and sustainable energy sources has never been more urgent. The Renewable Energy Directive (RED) is a crucial policy framework that aims to promote the use of renewable energy, specifically in the realm of biofuels. This subchapter will delve into the key aspects of RED and its significance in shaping the future of biofuels.

The Renewable Energy Directive was first introduced by the European Union (EU) in 2009 and has since undergone revisions to align with evolving environmental goals. The main objective of RED is to reduce greenhouse gas emissions and dependence on fossil fuels by increasing the share of renewable energy in the EU's energy mix. It sets binding targets for member states to ensure that 20% of the EU's final energy consumption comes from renewable sources by 2020, with a further target of at least 32% by 2030.

Under RED, biofuels play a vital role in the renewable energy transition. Biofuels are derived from organic materials such as crops, agricultural residues, and waste, making them a sustainable alternative to conventional fossil fuels. The directive sets specific criteria for these biofuels, ensuring they contribute to emissions reductions and do not cause adverse effects on land use, biodiversity, or food production.

One of the key provisions of RED is the implementation of sustainability criteria for biofuels. This mandates that biofuels must achieve a minimum greenhouse gas savings threshold compared to fossil fuels. Additionally, RED encourages the use of advanced biofuels, which have even higher sustainability standards and significantly lower greenhouse gas emissions.

The directive also promotes the development of bioenergy from waste and residues, as these resources are abundant and readily available. By utilizing waste materials for biofuel production, RED helps to minimize waste disposal while contributing to the circular economy.

Furthermore, RED encourages investment in research and innovation for the advancement of biofuels. It supports the development of second-generation biofuels, which can be produced from non-food crops or agricultural residues, reducing the potential conflicts between biofuel production and food security.

In conclusion, the Renewable Energy Directive (RED) is a crucial policy framework that aims to accelerate the transition towards renewable energy, specifically in the realm of biofuels. By setting binding targets, implementing sustainability criteria, and promoting research and innovation, RED plays a pivotal role in shaping a sustainable and environmentally friendly future. As individuals and communities, we can support the objectives of RED by advocating for renewable energy policies and actively choosing biofuels as a greener alternative. Together, we can fuel the future with clean and sustainable energy sources, mitigating the impacts of climate change and preserving our planet for future generations.

Sustainability Criteria for Biofuels

In recent years, there has been a growing interest in finding alternative sources of energy to mitigate the negative impacts of fossil fuels on the environment and reduce our dependence on them. Biofuels have emerged as a promising solution, offering a cleaner and more sustainable energy source. However, not all biofuels are created equal. To ensure that biofuels truly contribute to a greener future, it is crucial to establish sustainability criteria that govern their production and use.

Sustainability criteria for biofuels are guidelines and standards that aim to assess the environmental, social, and economic impacts of biofuel production. These criteria are essential for making informed decisions regarding the adoption and promotion of biofuels. By adhering to these guidelines, biofuel producers can minimize their carbon footprint and ensure that their operations are socially and economically responsible.

Environmental sustainability is a key aspect of biofuel production. It is crucial to evaluate the impact of biofuel feedstock cultivation on land use, biodiversity, and water resources. Sustainable biofuels should not contribute to deforestation or require the conversion of valuable ecosystems, such as forests or wetlands, into agricultural land. Additionally, the production process should minimize greenhouse gas emissions and water consumption, while maximizing energy efficiency.

Social sustainability criteria address the potential social impacts of biofuel production. It is important to consider the welfare of local communities and ensure that biofuel production does not negatively affect food security, land rights, or labor conditions. The biofuel industry should also promote fair trade practices and respect indigenous rights.

Economic sustainability involves evaluating the economic viability of biofuel production. It is crucial to assess the cost-effectiveness and market competitiveness of biofuels compared to fossil fuels. Additionally, biofuel production should contribute to rural development and create employment opportunities.

Implementing sustainability criteria for biofuels requires collaboration between governments, industry stakeholders, and environmental organizations. Transparent certification systems, such as the Roundtable on Sustainable Biomaterials (RSB) and the International Sustainability and Carbon Certification (ISCC), have been established to ensure compliance with these criteria and provide confidence to consumers.

By adopting and adhering to sustainability criteria, the biofuel industry can play a significant role in reducing greenhouse gas emissions, conserving natural resources, and promoting a more sustainable energy future. As consumers, it is crucial to be aware of these criteria and support biofuel producers who prioritize sustainability. Together, we can fuel the future with biofuels that are truly beneficial for the environment, society, and the economy.

Biofuel Policies in Developing Countries

In recent years, the global demand for energy has been increasing rapidly, resulting in a rise in greenhouse gas emissions and environmental degradation. To combat these issues, many countries are turning to biofuels as a sustainable alternative to fossil fuels. Developing countries, in particular, have recognized the potential benefits of biofuels and are implementing various policies and regulations to promote their production and use.

Biofuel policies in developing countries are driven by multiple factors, including energy security, rural development, and environmental sustainability. These policies aim to reduce dependency on imported fossil fuels, create new economic opportunities in rural areas, and mitigate the impact of climate change. By promoting the production and use of biofuels, governments seek to diversify their energy sources and foster sustainable development.

One common policy approach in developing countries is the implementation of biofuel mandates or blending targets. These mandates require a certain percentage of biofuels to be blended with conventional fuels, such as gasoline or diesel. By setting these targets, governments create a stable market for biofuels and incentivize investment in their production. Additionally, these policies help to reduce greenhouse gas emissions and improve air quality.

Another key aspect of biofuel policies in developing countries is the promotion of sustainable feedstock production. Feedstocks, such as corn, sugarcane, and palm oil, are used to produce biofuels. However, the cultivation of these crops can have negative environmental and social impacts, such as deforestation and land grabbing. To address these concerns, governments are introducing regulations to ensure that biofuel feedstocks are produced sustainably, without causing harm to the environment or local communities.

In addition to mandates and sustainable feedstock production, other policy measures include tax incentives, research and development funding, and capacity building programs. These initiatives aim to stimulate investment in biofuel technology, improve production efficiency, and enhance the overall competitiveness of the biofuel industry in developing countries.

While biofuel policies in developing countries hold great potential, challenges and opportunities exist. It is crucial to strike a balance between promoting biofuel production and addressing potential negative impacts on food security, land use, and biodiversity. Additionally, engaging with stakeholders, including local communities, farmers, and industry players, is essential for the successful implementation of these policies.

In conclusion, biofuel policies in developing countries play a vital role in transitioning towards a more sustainable future. These policies aim to reduce reliance on fossil fuels, create economic opportunities, and mitigate climate change. However, careful planning, monitoring, and evaluation are required to ensure that biofuel production and use are sustainable and beneficial to all stakeholders. By implementing effective policies, developing countries can harness the potential of biofuels and contribute to a greener and more sustainable energy sector.

Brazil

Brazil is a leading player in the biofuel industry and has garnered global attention for its successful implementation of biofuel policies and regulations. In this subchapter, we will explore the biofuel landscape in Brazil, highlighting its significant achievements and the reasons behind its success.

Brazil has long been recognized for its abundant natural resources, including vast amounts of arable land and a favorable climate for growing crops. These factors have created the perfect conditions for the production of biofuels, particularly ethanol. In fact, Brazil is the world's largest producer and exporter of ethanol, primarily derived from sugarcane.

The success of Brazil's biofuel industry can be attributed to a combination of governmental support, technological advancements, and favorable market conditions. In the 1970s, the Brazilian government implemented a series of policies aimed at reducing the country's dependence on imported oil. This included the introduction of the Proálcool program, which promoted the production and consumption of ethanol as a substitute for gasoline.

The Proálcool program was a resounding success, leading to a significant increase in ethanol production and a decrease in the country's reliance on fossil fuels. Today, ethanol accounts for over 40% of Brazil's total energy consumption in the transportation sector.

One of the key factors that sets Brazil apart from other countries in the biofuel industry is its efficient production process. Brazilian ethanol is produced from sugarcane, which is not only a highly efficient feedstock but also provides valuable co-products such as bagasse, a biomass that can be used for electricity generation. This integrated approach ensures maximum utilization of resources and minimizes waste.

Furthermore, Brazil has invested heavily in research and development to improve the efficiency of biofuel production. This has led to advancements in sugarcane breeding, fermentation processes, and the development of second-generation biofuels derived from agricultural residues and lignocellulosic materials.

Importantly, Brazil has also prioritized sustainable practices in its biofuel industry. The government imposes strict regulations to ensure that biofuel production does not lead to deforestation or the destruction of natural habitats. This commitment to sustainability has earned Brazil international recognition and positioned it as a global leader in responsible biofuel production.

In conclusion, Brazil's biofuel industry serves as a prime example of how effective policies, technological advancements, and sustainable practices can contribute to the success of the biofuel sector. The country's experience offers valuable insights for other nations looking to develop their own biofuel industries and reduce their reliance on fossil fuels.

Indonesia

Indonesia: Harnessing the Potential of Biofuels

Introduction:
Indonesia, a sprawling archipelago located in Southeast Asia, is a nation teeming with vast biodiversity and abundant natural resources. With a population of over 270 million people, Indonesia faces numerous challenges in meeting its energy demands while ensuring sustainable development. In recent years, the country has recognized the potential of biofuels as a viable alternative to fossil fuels, leading to the implementation of various policies and regulations aimed at harnessing the power of bioenergy.

1. Rich Agricultural Resources:
Indonesia boasts an array of fertile lands, making it an ideal candidate for biofuel production. The nation is blessed with vast plantations, primarily cultivating palm oil, sugarcane, and other crops suitable for bioenergy production. These resources provide a solid foundation for the development of a robust biofuel industry.

2. Biofuel Policies:
Recognizing the importance of reducing greenhouse gas emissions and promoting energy security, Indonesia has implemented comprehensive biofuel policies. The government introduced the Biofuel Mandatory Program in 2006, requiring a minimum biofuel blend in transportation fuels. This initiative has not only reduced the nation's dependence on imported oil but has also created new opportunities for rural communities engaged in biofuel production.

3. Palm Oil and Biodiesel:
Palm oil, a versatile crop widely cultivated in Indonesia, plays a crucial

role in the country's biofuel sector. Biodiesel, a renewable fuel derived from palm oil, is gaining popularity as a cleaner alternative to traditional diesel. The government has taken significant steps to promote biodiesel production, including the establishment of the Indonesian Palm Oil Board and the implementation of the B20 policy, which mandates a 20% palm oil-based biodiesel blend in diesel fuel.

4. Challenges and Opportunities: While Indonesia has made significant strides in biofuel development, challenges remain. Issues such as land use conflicts, deforestation, and sustainability concerns surrounding palm oil cultivation demand careful attention. However, these challenges also present opportunities for innovation and the implementation of sustainable practices, such as the adoption of advanced technologies and the cultivation of alternative feedstocks.

Conclusion:

Indonesia's commitment to biofuels demonstrates its determination to address energy security, reduce carbon emissions, and promote rural development. By capitalizing on its rich agricultural resources, particularly palm oil, Indonesia has positioned itself as a regional leader in the biofuel sector. The nation's biofuel policies and regulations provide a framework for sustainable development and serve as an inspiration for other countries seeking to transition to cleaner and more renewable energy sources.

India

India's Biofuel Journey: Paving the Way for a Sustainable Future

India, a land of rich cultural heritage and diversity, is not only a bustling economic powerhouse but also a frontrunner in the field of biofuels. With a population of over 1.3 billion, this subcontinent has recognized the importance of sustainable energy sources and has made significant strides in promoting the use of biofuels. In this subchapter, we delve into India's successful biofuel policies and regulations, shedding light on the country's efforts to create a greener and more sustainable future.

India's biofuel journey began in the early 2000s when the government realized the need to reduce its dependency on fossil fuels and mitigate the adverse effects of climate change. The introduction of the National Biofuel Policy in 2009 was a landmark moment, as it laid the foundation for the development and promotion of biofuels in the country. This policy aimed to blend biofuels with conventional fuels, reducing greenhouse gas emissions and promoting rural development by utilizing agricultural waste.

One of the key biofuels promoted in India is ethanol, derived from sugarcane molasses. The government has implemented the Ethanol Blending Program, which mandates the blending of ethanol with petrol, gradually increasing the percentage over time. This initiative not only reduces carbon emissions but also benefits farmers by creating an additional market for their sugarcane crops. Moreover, the country has set ambitious targets to achieve 20% ethanol blending by 2025, further reinforcing its commitment to sustainable energy.

Another significant biofuel in India's arsenal is biodiesel, primarily produced from non-edible oilseeds such as jatropha and pongamia. The government has introduced the Biodiesel Purchase Policy, which ensures a minimum support price for biodiesel, guaranteeing a market for the farmers. This policy has motivated farmers to cultivate non-edible oil crops, contributing to rural development and reducing the country's reliance on imported fossil fuels.

India's biofuel policies are not limited to ethanol and biodiesel alone; the government has also encouraged the production and utilization of biogas, biomethanol, and bio-CNG. These alternative fuels have diverse applications, from cooking gas to transportation fuel, and play a crucial role in reducing pollution and improving energy security.

Furthermore, India has been actively promoting research and development in biofuels, with a focus on advanced biofuels derived from non-food feedstocks. The country has established Bioenergy Research Centers and funded various projects to explore innovative technologies and processes for biofuel production.

In conclusion, India's biofuel journey is an inspiring tale of sustainable development and environmental stewardship. Through its well-crafted policies and regulations, the country has successfully harnessed the potential of biofuels, reducing carbon emissions, improving rural livelihoods, and paving the way for a greener and more sustainable future. As India continues to innovate and invest in biofuels, it sets an example for nations worldwide, showcasing the transformative power of renewable energy sources in combating climate change and ensuring a cleaner planet for future generations.

Chapter 5: Environmental and Social Impacts of Biofuels

Greenhouse Gas Emissions Reduction Potential

In recent decades, the increasing concern about climate change and its detrimental effects on the environment has led to a global focus on reducing greenhouse gas emissions. One sector that has gained significant attention in this regard is biofuels. Biofuels, derived from renewable organic materials such as plants, offer a promising solution to mitigate greenhouse gas emissions and transition towards a more sustainable future.

The potential for greenhouse gas emissions reduction through the use of biofuels is enormous. Unlike conventional fossil fuels, which release carbon dioxide into the atmosphere when burned, biofuels are considered carbon-neutral or even carbon-negative. This means that the amount of carbon dioxide released during their combustion is roughly equal to the amount of carbon dioxide absorbed by the plants during their growth. As a result, biofuels have the potential to significantly reduce net greenhouse gas emissions.

One of the key factors contributing to the greenhouse gas emissions reduction potential of biofuels is their ability to replace fossil fuels in various sectors. Transportation, for instance, is a major contributor to greenhouse gas emissions globally. By blending biofuels with gasoline or diesel, we can reduce the carbon footprint of transportation and decrease overall emissions. Furthermore, biofuels can be used in other sectors such as aviation and shipping, which are traditionally heavily reliant on fossil fuels.

Another aspect that enhances the greenhouse gas emissions reduction potential of biofuels is the cultivation of feedstock. Certain crops, such as switchgrass, Miscanthus, and algae, have a higher photosynthetic efficiency and can absorb more carbon dioxide from the atmosphere compared to traditional crops. Additionally, sustainable farming practices and the use of agricultural residues can further enhance the carbon sequestration potential of biofuel feedstocks.

It is important to note that while biofuels offer significant greenhouse gas emissions reduction potential, it is crucial to ensure sustainable production practices. The cultivation of feedstock should not lead to deforestation or the conversion of valuable ecosystems. Moreover, the overall life cycle analysis of biofuels, including the production, transportation, and distribution aspects, should be taken into account to accurately assess their environmental impact.

In conclusion, biofuels have tremendous potential to reduce greenhouse gas emissions and play a crucial role in fueling the future. By replacing conventional fossil fuels and utilizing sustainable feedstock cultivation practices, biofuels can significantly contribute to global efforts in combating climate change. However, it is imperative to implement robust policies and regulations that promote the sustainable production and utilization of biofuels to maximize their environmental benefits. Let us embrace the potential of biofuels and work towards a greener and more sustainable future for all.

Land Use Change and Deforestation

Introduction:

The issue of land use change and deforestation has become increasingly significant in the context of biofuels. As the world strives to reduce dependence on fossil fuels and transition to more sustainable energy sources, the production of biofuels has emerged as a promising alternative. However, the expansion of biofuel crops often leads to land use change, which can result in deforestation and environmental degradation. This subchapter aims to provide an overview of the relationship between land use change, deforestation, and biofuel production, while emphasizing the need for sustainable practices in the biofuel industry.

Land Use Change and Biofuels:

Biofuels, such as ethanol and biodiesel, are derived from renewable biomass sources, including agricultural crops, trees, and waste materials. To meet the growing demand for biofuels, extensive land is often converted for the cultivation of biofuel feedstocks. This land use change can involve clearing forests, draining wetlands, or displacing food crops, leading to biodiversity loss, increased greenhouse gas emissions, and soil degradation.

Deforestation and its Consequences:

Deforestation, primarily driven by agricultural expansion, contributes to approximately 10% of global greenhouse gas emissions. Forests play a crucial role in carbon sequestration, maintenance of biodiversity, and regulation of regional climates. Their destruction not only releases stored carbon but also disrupts ecosystems, leading to the loss of countless plant and animal species. Moreover, deforestation can exacerbate climate change, disrupt water cycles, and impact local communities that depend on forests for their livelihoods.

Sustainable Solutions:

Recognizing the environmental consequences of land use change and deforestation, sustainable practices are essential for the biofuel industry. Governments, policymakers, and industry stakeholders should work towards implementing policies and regulations that prioritize the protection of forests, wetlands, and other ecosystems. This can be achieved through the promotion of sustainable land management practices, such as agroforestry and reforestation, which can help balance the need for biofuel production with the preservation of natural habitats.

In addition, the development of advanced technologies, such as cellulosic biofuels that utilize non-food biomass, can reduce the pressure on arable land and minimize deforestation. It is crucial to conduct thorough environmental impact assessments and prioritize the use of degraded or abandoned lands for biofuel cultivation.

Conclusion:

Land use change and deforestation are significant challenges associated with the production of biofuels. As the world seeks to transition to more sustainable energy sources, it is essential to address these issues effectively. By adopting sustainable practices, promoting the use of advanced technologies, and implementing robust policies and regulations, the biofuel industry can contribute to reducing greenhouse gas emissions while protecting valuable ecosystems. Together, we can ensure that biofuels play a positive role in fueling the future without compromising the health of our planet.

Water Consumption and Pollution

In the pursuit of sustainable energy sources, the development and production of biofuels have gained significant traction. Biofuels, derived from organic materials such as crops or waste, offer a promising alternative to fossil fuels. However, it is crucial to understand the impact of biofuel production on water consumption and pollution.

Water consumption is a critical aspect of biofuel production. The cultivation and processing of crops for biofuel production require substantial amounts of water. For instance, corn-based ethanol production necessitates significant irrigation to support crop growth. This high water demand can strain local water resources, especially in areas already facing water scarcity issues. It is essential to adopt sustainable agricultural practices and efficient irrigation systems to minimize the water footprint of biofuel production.

Furthermore, biofuel production can also contribute to water pollution. The use of fertilizers and pesticides in crop cultivation can result in runoff, contaminating nearby water bodies. This pollution can harm aquatic ecosystems, affecting aquatic life and biodiversity. Additionally, biofuel production often involves various processing steps, such as fermentation and distillation, which generate wastewater containing organic matter and chemicals. Proper treatment and management of this wastewater are crucial to prevent its release into waterways, ensuring the preservation of water quality.

To address these challenges, policymakers and biofuel producers must implement strategies that minimize water consumption and pollution. This includes promoting the use of drought-tolerant crops that require less irrigation, implementing precision agriculture techniques to optimize water usage, and adopting integrated pest management practices to reduce the need for harmful chemicals.

Additionally, investing in research and development of advanced biofuel technologies can lead to more efficient production processes, thereby reducing water requirements. This includes exploring alternative feedstocks that do not compete with food production and have lower water demands.

Furthermore, regulatory frameworks and incentives should be established to encourage sustainable water management practices in the biofuel industry. This can include establishing water usage limits for biofuel production facilities, promoting water recycling and reuse, and implementing stricter wastewater treatment standards.

In conclusion, water consumption and pollution are significant considerations in the production of biofuels. As the world seeks to transition to renewable energy sources, it is essential to understand and mitigate the potential environmental impacts associated with biofuel production. By adopting sustainable practices, investing in research and development, and implementing effective regulations, we can ensure that biofuels contribute to a cleaner and more sustainable future without compromising our water resources.

Food Security and Agricultural Practices

In today's rapidly changing world, food security has become a critical concern for every individual. As the global population continues to grow, the demand for food is set to increase significantly. However, ensuring food security is not just about producing enough food to feed everyone, but also about doing so in a sustainable and environmentally friendly manner.

This subchapter aims to shed light on the vital link between food security and agricultural practices, specifically in the context of biofuels. Biofuels, derived from organic materials such as crops and agricultural waste, have gained significant attention as a potential alternative to fossil fuels. While biofuels offer the promise of reducing greenhouse gas emissions and promoting energy independence, their production can have both positive and negative impacts on food security and agricultural practices.

On the positive side, biofuel production can drive agricultural development, particularly in rural areas. Farmers can diversify their income sources by growing energy crops alongside traditional food crops. This can lead to increased incomes and improved livelihoods, contributing to poverty reduction and food security. Additionally, biofuel production can create job opportunities and stimulate economic growth in regions that heavily rely on agriculture.

However, there are also concerns that the widespread cultivation of energy crops for biofuels may compete with food production, leading to land-use conflicts and rising food prices. This has the potential to disproportionately impact vulnerable populations in developing countries, where access to food is already a challenge. Moreover, the expansion of biofuel feedstock cultivation can result in deforestation, loss of biodiversity, and increased water usage, jeopardizing the sustainability of agricultural practices.

To strike a balance between biofuel production and food security, it is crucial to implement sustainable agricultural practices. This includes promoting the use of marginal lands for energy crop cultivation, using advanced farming techniques to increase crop productivity, and investing in research and development to enhance the efficiency of biofuel production processes. Additionally, policymakers must ensure that appropriate regulations and incentives are in place to prevent the negative impacts of biofuel production on food security.

In conclusion, food security and agricultural practices are intrinsically linked to the development and implementation of biofuel policies and regulations. Achieving food security while promoting biofuels requires a careful balance between the potential benefits and the potential risks associated with biofuel production. By adopting sustainable agricultural practices and implementing appropriate policies, we can ensure that biofuels play a positive role in our future, contributing to both energy security and food security for all.

Social and Economic Implications

In recent years, the world has witnessed a growing interest in biofuels as a means to address both environmental and economic challenges. As our dependence on fossil fuels continues to contribute to climate change and geopolitical conflicts, the search for renewable energy sources has become more urgent than ever. Biofuels, derived from organic matter such as crops and agricultural waste, offer a promising alternative that can potentially reduce greenhouse gas emissions and enhance energy security. However, the adoption and implementation of biofuel policies and regulations entail certain social and economic implications that need to be thoroughly examined.

From a social standpoint, the widespread use of biofuels has the potential to bring about significant changes in various aspects of our lives. One of the most notable impacts is the potential for rural development. As biofuel production often relies on agricultural feedstocks, it can provide new opportunities for farmers and rural communities. By diversifying their income sources and promoting sustainable practices, biofuel production can help revitalize rural economies and reduce poverty levels. Additionally, the establishment of biofuel industries may create new job opportunities, particularly in regions with high agricultural potential.

However, it is essential to consider the potential social risks associated with biofuel production. The large-scale cultivation of biofuel feedstock crops can lead to land-use changes, which may result in deforestation, habitat destruction, and displacement of indigenous communities. Therefore, it is crucial to develop sustainable land-use practices that minimize the negative impacts on ecosystems and local communities. Additionally, the food versus fuel debate should be carefully addressed, as the diversion of agricultural crops for biofuel production may raise concerns about food security and affordability.

On the economic front, biofuel policies and regulations can have far-reaching consequences. The development of a biofuel industry can contribute to energy diversification and reduce reliance on fossil fuel imports, potentially enhancing energy security. Moreover, biofuel production can create new revenue streams and stimulate economic growth, particularly in countries heavily dependent on oil imports. By investing in biofuel research, development, and infrastructure, nations can foster innovation and create a competitive advantage in the emerging bioenergy market.

Nevertheless, the economic viability of biofuels remains a crucial consideration. The cost-effectiveness of biofuel production heavily depends on factors such as feedstock availability, technological advancements, and government support. Additionally, the fluctuating prices of fossil fuels can impact the competitiveness of biofuels. Therefore, it is vital to implement effective policies and incentives that promote sustainable biofuel production while ensuring economic feasibility.

In conclusion, the social and economic implications of biofuel policies and regulations are multifaceted and deserve careful consideration. While biofuels hold great potential for reducing greenhouse gas emissions, enhancing energy security, and supporting rural development, it is essential to address the associated challenges. By implementing sustainable land-use practices, promoting job creation, and ensuring economic viability, biofuels can play a significant role in fueling the future and transitioning towards a more sustainable and resilient energy system. However, a comprehensive approach that balances social, economic, and environmental considerations is crucial to harness the full potential of biofuels and create a more prosperous and equitable future for all.

Chapter 6: Challenges and Opportunities in Biofuel Policy Implementation

Technological and Infrastructural Challenges

The widespread adoption of biofuels as a viable alternative to fossil fuels has gained significant attention in recent years. As the world continues to grapple with the detrimental effects of climate change and the depletion of finite energy resources, the need for sustainable and cleaner energy solutions has become paramount. However, the successful integration of biofuels into our energy mix is not without its fair share of technological and infrastructural challenges.

One of the primary technological challenges in the biofuels industry is the development of efficient and cost-effective production methods. The production of biofuels requires the conversion of biomass, such as agricultural crops, waste materials, or algae, into usable fuel. This process, known as biomass conversion, is still in its nascent stages and faces several hurdles. Researchers and engineers are working tirelessly to improve conversion technologies, such as pyrolysis, fermentation, and gasification, to increase fuel yields, reduce production costs, and enhance overall efficiency.

Furthermore, the infrastructural challenges associated with biofuel adoption cannot be overlooked. Unlike traditional fossil fuel infrastructure, which is well-established and widely accessible, the infrastructure required for biofuel production, storage, and distribution is still lacking in many parts of the world. Developing countries, in particular, face significant hurdles in establishing the necessary infrastructure due to limited financial resources and technical expertise. Therefore, substantial investments in biofuel infrastructure are crucial to ensure the seamless integration of biofuels into existing energy systems.

Moreover, the transportation sector poses unique infrastructural challenges for biofuels. Most automobiles currently on the road are designed to run on gasoline or diesel, making it necessary to retrofit engines or design new vehicles capable of utilizing biofuels efficiently. This transition requires substantial investments in research and development, as well as collaboration between automakers, biofuel producers, and regulatory bodies. Additionally, the establishment of an extensive network of biofuel refueling stations is vital to facilitate the widespread adoption of biofuels in the transportation sector.

In conclusion, while biofuels hold immense potential to mitigate climate change and reduce our reliance on fossil fuels, several technological and infrastructural challenges must be addressed. The development of efficient and cost-effective production methods, establishment of robust biofuel infrastructure, and adaptation of vehicles to run on biofuels are critical steps towards realizing a sustainable and cleaner energy future. However, overcoming these challenges requires a collective effort from governments, industry stakeholders, and the scientific community. Only through effective collaboration and investment can we successfully fuel the future with biofuels.

Economic Considerations and Market Dynamics

The world is facing an increasing demand for sustainable and renewable energy sources due to the pressing need to reduce greenhouse gas emissions and mitigate climate change. Biofuels have emerged as a viable alternative to fossil fuels, offering a promising solution to meet these challenges. However, understanding the economic considerations and market dynamics that surround biofuels is crucial for effectively implementing policies and regulations in this rapidly evolving industry.

One of the key economic considerations of biofuels is their cost-effectiveness compared to traditional fossil fuels. While biofuels have the potential to reduce carbon emissions and dependence on imported oil, their production costs can often be higher than those of conventional fuels. Factors such as feedstock availability, processing technologies, and economies of scale play a significant role in determining the cost competitiveness of biofuels. Policymakers and industry stakeholders must carefully evaluate the economic viability of biofuel projects to ensure their long-term sustainability.

Market dynamics also influence the success of biofuels. The development and growth of biofuel markets depend on several factors, including government policies, market incentives, and consumer demand. Favorable policies, such as tax credits and renewable fuel standards, can create a conducive environment for biofuel production and stimulate investment in the sector. Additionally, increasing consumer awareness and demand for sustainable and eco-friendly products can drive market growth and create opportunities for biofuel producers.

However, market dynamics can be complex and subject to fluctuations. Changes in government policies, shifts in energy prices, and advancements in alternative technologies can all impact the demand for biofuels. Therefore, it is essential to carefully analyze market trends and anticipate potential challenges to ensure the stability and growth of the biofuel industry.

Furthermore, understanding the global biofuel market dynamics is crucial. Different countries have varying levels of biofuel production and consumption, as well as different regulatory frameworks. International trade policies and agreements also play a significant role in shaping the global biofuel market. A comprehensive understanding of these dynamics is essential for policymakers, industry stakeholders, and investors to navigate the complexities of the global biofuel landscape.

In conclusion, economic considerations and market dynamics are critical factors in shaping the future of biofuels. Policymakers, industry stakeholders, and investors must carefully evaluate the cost-effectiveness, market demand, and global dynamics of biofuels to ensure their successful implementation. By fostering a favorable economic environment and understanding market trends, the biofuel industry can thrive and contribute significantly to a sustainable and low-carbon future.

Stakeholder Engagement and Public Perception

In the rapidly evolving world of biofuels, one crucial aspect that cannot be overlooked is stakeholder engagement and public perception. As the demand for alternative fuel sources continues to grow, it becomes imperative for policymakers, industry leaders, and researchers to actively involve all stakeholders and address any concerns or misconceptions surrounding biofuels.

Stakeholder engagement is the process of involving individuals, organizations, and communities that have a vested interest or are affected by biofuel policies and regulations. These stakeholders include farmers, environmentalists, energy companies, consumers, and government agencies, among others. Engaging with these diverse groups ensures that their voices are heard, and their concerns are taken into account when formulating biofuel policies.

One of the key challenges faced in stakeholder engagement is addressing public perception. Many people still hold misconceptions about biofuels, which can hinder their acceptance and adoption. Some critics argue that biofuels compete with food production, leading to land degradation and increased food prices. Others express concerns about the environmental impact of biofuel production, such as deforestation or water pollution.

To overcome these challenges, a comprehensive communication strategy is required. This strategy should include educating the public about the benefits and potential drawbacks of biofuels, addressing misconceptions, and providing transparent information about the biofuel production process. It is critical to highlight the positive aspects of biofuels, such as their potential to reduce greenhouse gas emissions, decrease reliance on fossil fuels, and promote rural development through the cultivation of biofuel feedstocks.

Furthermore, engaging with stakeholders should not be limited to information dissemination alone. It is equally important to actively involve them in the decision-making process and seek their input. This can be done through public consultations, workshops, and partnerships with community organizations. By involving stakeholders in the early stages of policy development, their concerns can be addressed, and better-informed decisions can be made.

Ultimately, effective stakeholder engagement and addressing public perception are essential for the successful implementation of biofuel policies and regulations. By actively involving all stakeholders and fostering a transparent dialogue, policymakers and industry leaders can build trust, gain support, and ensure the long-term viability of biofuels as a sustainable alternative to traditional fossil fuels.

In conclusion, stakeholder engagement and public perception play a significant role in shaping the future of biofuels. By incorporating the concerns and perspectives of various stakeholders and actively addressing public misconceptions, policymakers and industry leaders can foster acceptance and support for biofuels. This will contribute to the transition towards a more sustainable and environmentally friendly energy system, ensuring a brighter future for all.

Future Opportunities and Potential Solutions

As the world grapples with the need for sustainable and clean energy sources, biofuels have emerged as a promising solution. In this subchapter, we will explore the future opportunities that biofuels present and delve into potential solutions to overcome existing challenges. Whether you are a biofuel enthusiast, an industry professional, or simply curious about renewable energy, this section will provide valuable insights into the future of biofuels.

The road ahead for biofuels is filled with immense potential. As the global demand for energy continues to rise, biofuels offer a sustainable alternative to fossil fuels. By harnessing the power of renewable resources such as biomass, algae, and agricultural waste, biofuels can significantly reduce greenhouse gas emissions and combat climate change. This presents a unique opportunity to transition towards a low-carbon economy while also creating new job opportunities and fostering economic growth.

One of the key future opportunities lies in technological advancements. Researchers and scientists are continually exploring innovative ways to enhance the production and efficiency of biofuels. From genetic engineering to improve crop yields, to the development of advanced conversion technologies, the biofuel industry is poised for significant breakthroughs. These advancements will not only increase the availability of biofuels but also make them more cost-effective and compatible with existing infrastructure.

Furthermore, biofuels hold the potential to revolutionize the transportation sector. As electric vehicles gain popularity, biofuels can serve as a complementary solution, particularly for long-haul trucks, aviation, and marine vessels. By blending biofuels with conventional fuels or exploring bio-based alternatives, we can reduce the carbon footprint of these industries and pave the way for a greener future.

However, several challenges must be overcome to fully harness the potential of biofuels. One such challenge is the availability of feedstock. Scaling up biofuel production requires a steady and sustainable supply of biomass, which can be influenced by factors such as land use conflicts, water scarcity, and competition with food crops. Finding innovative solutions to these issues, such as utilizing marginal lands and adopting sustainable farming practices, will be crucial.

Another challenge lies in policy and regulatory frameworks. Governments around the world need to provide long-term support and incentives to encourage investment in biofuel production and infrastructure. This includes establishing clear and stable policies, implementing favorable tax regimes, and promoting research and development in the field.

In conclusion, the future of biofuels holds tremendous promise. By capitalizing on technological advancements, addressing challenges related to feedstock availability, and implementing supportive policies, we can unlock the full potential of biofuels. This will not only contribute to a more sustainable energy future but also foster economic growth and mitigate the impacts of climate change. As individuals, industry professionals, and policymakers, we all have a role to play in fueling the future of biofuels. Let us embrace this opportunity and work together towards a greener and more prosperous world.

Chapter 7: Case Studies on Biofuel Policies and Regulations

Case Study 1: United States' Renewable Fuel Standard

Introduction:
In this chapter, we will delve into a fascinating case study focusing on the United States' Renewable Fuel Standard (RFS). The RFS is a vital policy that promotes the use of renewable fuels, particularly biofuels, in the transportation sector. Understanding the intricacies of this policy will enable us to grasp the significance of biofuel policies and regulations in the broader context of fueling the future.

Background:
The United States, like many other nations, faces challenges related to energy security, climate change, and the need to reduce dependence on fossil fuels. Biofuels have emerged as a promising alternative due to their potential to reduce greenhouse gas emissions and promote sustainable development. The RFS was introduced in response to these challenges, aiming to increase the production and use of biofuels in the country.

Evolution of the RFS:
This subchapter will provide a comprehensive overview of the RFS's evolution over the years. Starting from its inception in 2005 under the Energy Policy Act, we will explore the subsequent amendments and updates that have shaped the policy's current form. By tracing its development, we can identify the motivations behind the changes and the impact they have had on biofuel production and consumption.

Implementation and Compliance:
Implementing the RFS poses unique challenges, as it involves

coordinating efforts between government agencies, fuel producers, and other stakeholders. This section will examine the mechanisms put in place to ensure compliance with the RFS mandates, such as the establishment of Renewable Identification Numbers (RINs) and the role of the Environmental Protection Agency (EPA). We will also discuss the controversies and debates surrounding compliance, including issues related to fraud and market manipulation.

Economic and Environmental Impacts:
The RFS has far-reaching economic and environmental implications. This chapter will explore the economic benefits and challenges associated with biofuel production, such as job creation, rural development, and the potential for reducing oil imports. Additionally, we will assess the environmental impacts of biofuel production, including carbon emissions, land use changes, and biodiversity concerns.

Lessons Learned and Future Outlook:
As we conclude this case study, we will reflect on the lessons learned from the United States' Renewable Fuel Standard. By analyzing the successes and failures of the policy, we can gain insights into the potential improvements and future directions for biofuel policies and regulations globally. We will also discuss emerging technologies and innovations that could shape the biofuel landscape in the coming years.

Conclusion:
The United States' Renewable Fuel Standard serves as an illuminating case study in understanding the complexities of biofuel policies and regulations. By exploring its evolution, implementation, impacts, and future outlook, we can develop a comprehensive understanding of the

challenges and opportunities associated with transitioning to a sustainable energy future. Whether you are an industry professional, policy maker, or simply interested in biofuels, this case study will provide valuable insights into the world of renewable fuel policies.

Case Study 2: European Union's Renewable Energy Directive

The European Union's Renewable Energy Directive (RED) is a crucial policy framework that has had a significant impact on the biofuel industry within the region. Introduced in 2009, the RED aimed to promote the use of renewable energy sources, reduce greenhouse gas emissions, and enhance energy security.

Biofuels, derived from organic matter such as crops and agricultural residues, have played a vital role in the EU's strategy to transition towards a more sustainable and low-carbon economy. The RED sets binding targets for member states to increase the share of renewable energy in transportation, with specific requirements for biofuels.

One of the key provisions of the RED is the establishment of a target to achieve a 10% share of renewable energy in the transport sector by 2020. To meet this target, member states have implemented various measures, including the blending of biofuels with conventional fossil fuels, promoting the use of advanced biofuels, and encouraging the development of sustainable feedstocks.

However, the RED has not been without its challenges. One issue that arose was the potential negative environmental and social impacts of biofuel production. Concerns were raised over the displacement of food crops, deforestation, and the use of unsustainable feedstocks, which could undermine the environmental benefits of biofuels. In response, the EU introduced sustainability criteria to ensure that biofuels used for compliance with the RED meet certain environmental and social standards.

Furthermore, the RED has also faced criticism for its indirect land-use change (ILUC) effects. ILUC refers to the phenomenon where the expansion of biofuel production leads to the conversion of land previously used for food or feed crops, resulting in indirect environmental consequences. To address this issue, the EU introduced ILUC factors, which account for the emissions associated with ILUC in the life-cycle analysis of biofuels.

Despite these challenges, the RED has been successful in promoting the growth of the biofuel industry in the European Union. It has provided a stable regulatory framework, incentivized investments in biofuel production, and encouraged innovation in advanced biofuels. The RED has also stimulated the development of sustainable feedstocks, such as waste and residues, which have the potential to further reduce the environmental impact of biofuels.

In conclusion, the European Union's Renewable Energy Directive has been a significant driver for the biofuel industry. While facing challenges related to sustainability and ILUC, the RED has successfully increased the share of renewable energy in transportation and supported the development of a more sustainable and low-carbon future. As the biofuel sector continues to evolve, the lessons learned from the RED can serve as a valuable guide for other regions and countries looking to implement similar policies.

Case Study 3: Brazil's Ethanol Program

Introduction:

In the pursuit of sustainable and environmentally friendly fuel alternatives, Brazil's ethanol program has emerged as a shining example. With its vast agricultural resources and a commitment to reducing carbon emissions, Brazil has successfully developed a thriving biofuel industry. This case study explores the history, implementation, and impact of Brazil's ethanol program, highlighting its significance in the global biofuel landscape.

History and Implementation:

Brazil's ethanol program traces its origins back to the 1970s when the country faced an energy crisis due to an overreliance on imported oil. This crisis prompted the government to explore alternative solutions, leading to the development of a national ethanol program. The program aimed to promote the use of sugarcane-based ethanol as a substitute for gasoline, leveraging Brazil's abundant sugarcane production.

The government provided substantial support, investing in research and development, creating incentives for farmers and industries, and establishing a comprehensive infrastructure for ethanol production and distribution. Additionally, flex-fuel vehicles capable of running on both gasoline and ethanol were introduced, encouraging consumer adoption.

Impact and Benefits:

Brazil's ethanol program has yielded significant environmental, economic, and social benefits. From an environmental standpoint, the program has resulted in a substantial reduction in carbon emissions.

Ethanol, as a renewable fuel source, emits significantly fewer greenhouse gases compared to traditional fossil fuels. It has also played a crucial role in reducing air pollution, leading to improved air quality in urban areas.

Economically, Brazil's ethanol program has boosted the country's energy independence, reducing its reliance on costly oil imports. This has had a positive impact on Brazil's trade balance and overall economic stability. The program has also created numerous employment opportunities, particularly in rural areas where sugarcane farming and ethanol production are concentrated.

Furthermore, Brazil's ethanol program has contributed to the development of a robust biofuel industry. The country has become a global leader in ethanol production, exporting significant quantities to other countries. This has not only generated revenue but also fostered technological advancements and knowledge sharing within the biofuel sector.

Conclusion:

Brazil's ethanol program stands as an exemplary model for the successful implementation of a biofuel initiative. It showcases how a combination of government support, investment in research and technology, and favorable policies can drive the adoption of sustainable fuel alternatives. The program's positive impact on the environment, economy, and society demonstrates the potential of biofuels to play a vital role in a sustainable and greener future.

Whether as a source of inspiration or a benchmark for other nations, Brazil's ethanol program offers valuable insights into the possibilities and challenges associated with biofuel initiatives. As the world seeks to reduce its dependence on fossil fuels and combat climate change, understanding and learning from successful programs like Brazil's can pave the way for a more sustainable energy future.

Case Study 4: Indonesia's Palm Oil-based Biofuel Initiative

Introduction:

In this chapter, we will delve into a fascinating case study that highlights the potential of biofuels in driving sustainable development and reducing greenhouse gas emissions. Indonesia, a country rich in palm oil production, has embarked on an ambitious biofuel initiative utilizing its abundant palm oil resources. This case study will shed light on the challenges faced, the strategies employed, and the outcomes achieved in Indonesia's palm oil-based biofuel initiative.

Background:

Indonesia, the world's largest producer of palm oil, recognized the need to reduce its dependence on fossil fuels and mitigate the adverse environmental impacts associated with them. With its vast palm oil plantations, the country saw an opportunity to leverage this resource to produce biofuels, thus reducing greenhouse gas emissions and promoting renewable energy.

Challenges:

The biofuel initiative faced several challenges, including the need for proper infrastructure, ensuring sustainable palm oil cultivation practices, and addressing concerns regarding deforestation and its impact on biodiversity. Additionally, the initiative required substantial investments and policy reforms to create a conducive environment for biofuel production and consumption.

Strategies:

To overcome these challenges, the Indonesian government implemented a comprehensive strategy that included the development of dedicated biofuel refineries, the promotion of sustainable palm oil cultivation practices, and the establishment of certification systems to ensure traceability and accountability. Furthermore, collaborations with international organizations and stakeholders were forged to enhance knowledge sharing and capacity building.

Outcomes:

Indonesia's palm oil-based biofuel initiative has yielded promising outcomes. The country has witnessed a significant increase in biofuel production, leading to a substantial reduction in greenhouse gas emissions. This initiative has also created new job opportunities in rural areas, contributing to poverty alleviation and economic growth. Furthermore, sustainable palm oil practices have been adopted, resulting in better land management and protection of biodiversity.

Conclusion:

Indonesia's palm oil-based biofuel initiative serves as an inspiring example of how a country can leverage its natural resources to address energy security, environmental concerns, and socio-economic development simultaneously. However, it is crucial to strike a balance between biofuel production and sustainability, ensuring that palm oil cultivation does not lead to deforestation or harm local communities. This case study underscores the importance of robust policies, infrastructure development, and international collaborations in fostering a sustainable biofuel industry. By learning from Indonesia's experiences, other countries can implement similar initiatives to transition towards a greener and more sustainable future.

Chapter 8: Evaluating the Effectiveness of Biofuel Policies and Regulations

Metrics for Assessing Policy Impact

In the ever-evolving world of biofuels, it is crucial to have a clear understanding of the impact of policies and regulations. Assessing the effectiveness of these measures is essential in order to make informed decisions and ensure the sustainable growth of the biofuels industry. In this subchapter, we will explore the various metrics that can be used to assess policy impact in the realm of biofuels.

One of the primary metrics for evaluating policy impact is greenhouse gas emissions reduction. Biofuels, when produced sustainably, have the potential to significantly reduce carbon emissions compared to fossil fuels. Policymakers must consider the overall reduction in greenhouse gas emissions achieved by implementing biofuel policies. This metric provides valuable insights into the environmental benefits and the overall contribution of biofuels to mitigating climate change.

Another important metric is energy security. Biofuels can play a vital role in reducing a country's dependence on fossil fuel imports, thus improving energy security. By assessing the extent to which biofuel policies contribute to energy diversification and independence, policymakers can gauge the effectiveness of these measures in addressing energy security concerns.

Economic metrics are also crucial for assessing policy impact. Job creation, economic growth, and investment in the biofuels sector are key indicators of the success of biofuel policies. Evaluating the number of jobs created and the economic benefits generated by the biofuels industry can help policymakers determine the effectiveness of policies in stimulating economic growth and fostering a sustainable biofuels market.

Furthermore, metrics related to technological advancements and innovation should be considered. Policies that encourage research and development in biofuel technologies can lead to breakthroughs in efficiency, cost-effectiveness, and sustainability. Assessing the level of technological progress achieved through policy implementation helps in identifying areas for improvement and directing future policy efforts towards fostering innovation in the biofuels sector.

Lastly, social metrics such as rural development and social equity should not be overlooked. Biofuel policies can have a significant impact on rural communities by creating employment opportunities and supporting local economies. Assessing the extent to which policies contribute to rural development and social equity ensures that the benefits of biofuels are shared equitably among different segments of society.

By utilizing these metrics, policymakers and stakeholders can assess the impact of biofuel policies and regulations comprehensively. This evaluation will enable them to identify successful strategies, rectify shortcomings, and make informed decisions to foster the sustainable growth of the biofuels industry. Ultimately, the goal is to create a future where biofuels play a central role in achieving a cleaner, more secure, and economically viable energy system for everyone.

Comparative Analysis of Biofuel Policies

In today's world, where sustainability and environmental concerns are of paramount importance, biofuels have emerged as a promising alternative to traditional fossil fuels. As governments and industries around the globe strive to reduce greenhouse gas emissions and promote cleaner energy sources, understanding the biofuel policies and regulations becomes crucial.

This subchapter aims to provide a comprehensive comparative analysis of biofuel policies implemented by various nations. By examining different approaches to biofuel production, distribution, and consumption, we can gain valuable insights into the effectiveness of these policies and identify best practices.

One of the primary factors influencing biofuel policies is the availability of feedstock. Different countries possess varying natural resources, such as corn, sugarcane, soybeans, or palm oil, which can be used as feedstock for biofuel production. By comparing the policies adopted by countries with different feedstock options, we can evaluate the impact of feedstock availability on biofuel production and the overall sustainability of the industry.

Moreover, the regulatory framework surrounding biofuel policies also plays a vital role in shaping the market. Some countries have implemented mandates or targets for the blending of biofuels with conventional fuels, while others offer incentives and subsidies to encourage investment in the biofuel sector. By analyzing the outcomes of these different approaches, we can identify the most effective strategies to promote the growth and adoption of biofuels.

Additionally, it is important to consider the socio-economic implications of biofuel policies. Biofuel production can have both positive and negative effects on local communities, such as job creation, land use changes, and food security concerns. By comparing policies that successfully address these issues, we can learn how to strike a balance between economic development and environmental sustainability.

This subchapter will provide real-world examples of biofuel policies from countries like Brazil, the United States, Germany, and Indonesia, among others. By examining the successes and challenges faced by these nations, readers will gain a comprehensive understanding of the complexities and nuances involved in formulating effective biofuel policies.

Whether you are a biofuel industry professional, an environmental enthusiast, or simply someone curious about the future of energy, this subchapter will equip you with the knowledge needed to navigate the dynamic landscape of biofuel policies. Join us as we delve into the comparative analysis of biofuel policies and explore the possibilities for a greener, more sustainable future.

Lessons Learned and Best Practices

In the ever-evolving world of biofuels, it is crucial to examine the lessons learned and best practices that have emerged over the years. As the demand for renewable energy sources continues to grow, the biofuels industry plays a vital role in addressing climate change and reducing greenhouse gas emissions. This subchapter aims to provide valuable insights and guidance for anyone interested in understanding biofuel policies and regulations, from industry professionals to policymakers and the general public.

One of the key lessons learned in the biofuels sector is the importance of clear and consistent policy frameworks. Historically, policy uncertainty has hindered investment and slowed the growth of the industry. Governments and regulatory bodies must provide stable and predictable policies to attract investments and promote long-term growth. By learning from past mistakes, policymakers can create an enabling environment that encourages innovation and incentivizes the adoption of biofuels.

Another crucial lesson is the need for comprehensive sustainability standards. Biofuels have the potential to deliver significant environmental benefits, but they must be produced sustainably to avoid unintended negative consequences. Best practices involve implementing robust certification systems that ensure biofuel feedstocks are sourced responsibly, without causing deforestation or biodiversity loss. Additionally, policies should promote the use of advanced technologies that maximize efficiency and minimize waste in biofuel production processes.

In terms of best practices, fostering collaboration and knowledge-sharing among stakeholders is paramount. The biofuels industry is multidimensional, involving farmers, researchers, policymakers, and private sector entities. By promoting open dialogue and cooperation, stakeholders can collectively address challenges and identify innovative solutions. Sharing best practices from successful biofuel initiatives can help accelerate the adoption of sustainable biofuel production methods globally.

Furthermore, continuous research and development are essential in advancing the biofuels industry. Investing in research can lead to breakthroughs in feedstock optimization, new production techniques, and improved energy conversion. Governments and industry players should allocate resources to support research institutions and encourage public-private partnerships that drive innovation.

Ultimately, understanding the lessons learned and best practices in the biofuels sector is crucial for shaping effective policies and regulations. By harnessing the potential of biofuels, we can reduce our dependence on fossil fuels, mitigate climate change impacts, and foster a sustainable future. Whether you are an industry professional or simply interested in biofuels, this subchapter provides valuable insights that can guide and inspire you to contribute to the growth and development of this vital renewable energy sector.

Recommendations for Future Policy Development

As the world grapples with the challenges of climate change and the need for sustainable energy sources, the role of biofuels cannot be understated. Biofuels, derived from organic matter such as crops and waste materials, have the potential to significantly reduce greenhouse gas emissions and dependence on fossil fuels. However, in order to fully harness the benefits of biofuels, it is crucial to develop effective policies and regulations that foster their growth and development. This subchapter aims to provide recommendations for future policy development in the field of biofuels.

1. Encourage Research and Development: Governments should invest in research and development of advanced biofuel technologies. This will not only enhance the efficiency of biofuel production but also address concerns related to land use, food security, and environmental impact. Financial incentives and grants should be provided to support innovative projects in this area.

2. Implement Clear and Consistent Regulations: Governments should establish clear and consistent regulations for biofuel production, distribution, and use. These regulations should address issues such as sustainability criteria, feedstock certification, greenhouse gas emissions, and land use change. By providing a stable regulatory environment, policymakers can foster investor confidence and attract private sector participation.

3. Promote International Cooperation: International cooperation and knowledge sharing are essential for the growth of the biofuel industry. Governments should collaborate with each other, sharing best practices, research findings, and policy experiences. This will help

create a global framework that facilitates the development and trade of sustainable biofuels.

4. Support Infrastructure Development: In order to facilitate the widespread use of biofuels, governments should invest in the development of necessary infrastructure. This includes building biofuel production facilities, expanding distribution networks, and promoting the availability of biofuel-compatible vehicles. Financial incentives and grants should be provided to encourage private sector participation in infrastructure development.

5. Create Market Incentives: Governments should create market incentives to encourage the use of biofuels. This can include tax breaks, subsidies, and mandates for blending biofuels with conventional fossil fuels. By creating a favorable market environment, policymakers can drive demand for biofuels and spur investment in their production.

In conclusion, the development of effective policies and regulations is crucial for the growth and success of the biofuel industry. By implementing the recommendations outlined in this subchapter, policymakers can create an enabling environment that fosters innovation, sustainability, and widespread adoption of biofuels. It is through concerted efforts and collaboration that we can fuel a greener and more sustainable future for all.

Chapter 9: The Future of Biofuel Policies and Regulations

Emerging Technologies and Biofuel Alternatives

In today's rapidly evolving world, where concerns about climate change and the depletion of fossil fuel resources are at the forefront of global discussions, emerging technologies and biofuel alternatives provide a glimmer of hope. The need for sustainable and renewable energy sources has never been more pressing, and biofuels offer a promising solution.

Biofuels are derived from organic matter, such as crops, agricultural waste, and algae. They can be used as a substitute for traditional fossil fuels, such as gasoline and diesel, in transportation and other energy-intensive sectors. The beauty of biofuels lies in their ability to reduce greenhouse gas emissions and mitigate environmental impact, while also providing a more sustainable energy option.

This subchapter delves into the exciting world of emerging technologies and biofuel alternatives, exploring the latest advancements, breakthroughs, and their implications for a cleaner, greener future. Whether you are a biofuel enthusiast, an environmentalist, or simply curious about the future of energy, this subchapter is for you.

We will explore various types of biofuels, such as ethanol, biodiesel, and biogas, and their production processes. Additionally, we will discuss the challenges and opportunities associated with biofuel production, including feedstock availability, land use considerations, and technological advancements.

One of the most promising emerging technologies in the field of biofuels is algae-based biofuel. Algae have the potential to produce significantly higher yields of biofuel compared to traditional crops, without competing with food production or requiring large amounts of arable land. We will delve into the science behind algae-based biofuel production, its scalability, and the potential it holds for revolutionizing the biofuel industry.

Furthermore, this subchapter will touch upon other emerging technologies, such as cellulosic biofuels, which utilize non-food feedstocks like agricultural waste and dedicated energy crops. These technologies have the potential to overcome some of the limitations faced by conventional biofuel production, making them a crucial part of the future biofuel landscape.

Ultimately, understanding emerging technologies and biofuel alternatives is essential for individuals, policymakers, and industries alike. It is only through a collective effort and a deeper understanding of these technologies that we can transition to a more sustainable and environmentally friendly future.

So, whether you are a biofuel enthusiast seeking the latest advancements or simply someone interested in the future of energy, this subchapter will provide you with valuable insights into the world of emerging technologies and biofuel alternatives. Join us on this exciting journey towards a cleaner, greener future!

Shifting Paradigms in Policy Approaches

In recent years, the global energy landscape has witnessed a significant transformation, with a growing emphasis on sustainable and renewable energy sources. This shift has given rise to the emergence of biofuels as a viable alternative to conventional fossil fuels. As governments and policymakers around the world recognize the urgent need to address climate change and reduce greenhouse gas emissions, biofuel policies and regulations have become a focal point in achieving these goals.

The subchapter "Shifting Paradigms in Policy Approaches" delves into the changing perspectives and strategies adopted by governments and policymakers in the realm of biofuel policies. This section aims to provide a comprehensive understanding of the evolving regulatory frameworks and their implications for the biofuel industry.

One of the key paradigms that has shifted in biofuel policies is the recognition of the multifaceted benefits that biofuels offer. Initially, policies focused primarily on reducing dependence on fossil fuels and enhancing energy security. However, as the understanding of climate change and its consequences deepened, policymakers began incorporating environmental considerations into biofuel policies. Today, biofuels are seen as a means to mitigate greenhouse gas emissions, promote sustainable land use practices, and contribute to the circular economy.

Another paradigm shift is the move towards a more holistic approach to biofuel policies. In the past, policies tended to focus on specific biofuel feedstocks, such as corn or sugarcane. However, recognizing the need for diverse and sustainable feedstock sources, policymakers are now adopting a technology-neutral approach. This approach encourages the development of a range of biofuel feedstocks, including advanced and second-generation options like algae, agricultural residues, and municipal waste.

Furthermore, there has been a shift from command-and-control regulatory approaches to market-based mechanisms. Governments are increasingly leveraging market forces to drive biofuel adoption by implementing policies such as renewable fuel standards, carbon pricing, and tax incentives. These market-based approaches not only create a level playing field for biofuels but also stimulate innovation and investment in the sector.

In conclusion, the subchapter "Shifting Paradigms in Policy Approaches" explores the changing landscape of biofuel policies and regulations. It highlights the growing recognition of the environmental benefits of biofuels, the shift towards a holistic approach, and the adoption of market-based mechanisms. Understanding these paradigm shifts is essential for a diverse audience, including policymakers, industry professionals, researchers, and anyone interested in the biofuel sector. By examining the evolving policy landscape, we can gain valuable insights into the future of biofuels and their role in fueling a sustainable future for all.

Global Collaboration and Harmonization Efforts

In today's interconnected world, the need for global collaboration and harmonization efforts in the realm of biofuels has become increasingly imperative. As nations strive to address the challenges posed by climate change and the depletion of fossil fuel reserves, the development and implementation of sustainable biofuel policies and regulations have gained significant momentum. This chapter explores the importance of global collaboration and harmonization efforts in shaping the future of biofuels.

Biofuels, derived from renewable sources such as biomass, offer a promising alternative to conventional fossil fuels. They have the potential to reduce greenhouse gas emissions, enhance energy security, and promote rural development. However, the biofuel sector is still in its nascent stages, and the lack of uniformity in policies and regulations across countries has hindered its growth and potential impact.

Global collaboration in the biofuel industry is crucial for several reasons. Firstly, it enables knowledge sharing and technology transfer, fostering innovation and advancements in biofuel production techniques. By collaborating with international partners, countries can learn from each other's successes and failures, accelerating the development of more efficient and sustainable biofuel technologies.

Secondly, harmonization efforts play a vital role in creating a level playing field for biofuel producers and investors. Discrepancies in regulations and standards can create trade barriers and market distortions. By aligning policies and regulations, countries can promote fair competition, facilitate international trade, and attract private sector investments in the biofuel industry.

Furthermore, global collaboration and harmonization efforts are essential in addressing sustainability concerns associated with biofuel production. For instance, the cultivation of feedstock crops for biofuels can lead to deforestation, habitat destruction, and food security issues. By working together, countries can establish common sustainability criteria and certification schemes, ensuring that biofuel production adheres to stringent environmental and social standards.

International organizations, such as the International Energy Agency (IEA), the United Nations Framework Convention on Climate Change (UNFCCC), and the Global Bioenergy Partnership (GBEP), play a pivotal role in facilitating global collaboration and harmonization efforts. These organizations provide platforms for dialogue, knowledge exchange, and the development of international biofuel frameworks.

In conclusion, global collaboration and harmonization efforts are indispensable for the growth and sustainability of the biofuel industry. By working together, countries can overcome barriers, foster innovation, and promote the widespread adoption of biofuels. It is through such collaborative efforts that we can fuel a cleaner and more sustainable future for all.

Sustainable Biofuel Pathways for a Greener Future

In recent years, the world has witnessed a growing concern regarding the adverse impacts of conventional fossil fuels on the environment and climate change. As a result, the search for alternative and sustainable energy sources has become an urgent priority. One such solution that has gained significant attention is biofuels - renewable energy sources derived from organic matter such as plants and agricultural waste. This subchapter explores the various sustainable biofuel pathways that hold the potential to pave the way for a greener future.

Biofuels offer several advantages over conventional fuels. Firstly, they are carbon-neutral, meaning they do not contribute to the net increase of greenhouse gas emissions. When biofuels are burned, they release carbon dioxide (CO_2) into the atmosphere, but this is offset by the CO_2 absorbed during the growth of the feedstock. This closed carbon cycle makes biofuels an attractive option in the fight against climate change.

One of the most promising sustainable biofuel pathways is the production of ethanol from biomass. Biomass can be derived from various sources, such as sugarcane, corn, or even algae. Ethanol, a type of alcohol, can be blended with gasoline to reduce the overall carbon footprint of transportation. Additionally, the by-products of ethanol production, such as bagasse or corn stover, can be used for power generation, further enhancing the sustainability of this pathway.

Another sustainable biofuel pathway is the production of biodiesel from vegetable oils, animal fats, or used cooking oil. Biodiesel can be used as a direct replacement or blended with diesel fuel, significantly reducing emissions of particulate matter and other harmful pollutants.

Moreover, the production of biodiesel creates opportunities for utilizing waste materials and reducing landfill waste.

To ensure the sustainability of biofuel pathways, it is crucial to consider the entire life cycle of the fuel, from feedstock cultivation to fuel distribution. This involves evaluating the environmental, social, and economic impacts associated with biofuel production. It is essential to strike a balance between the need for biofuel production and the potential risks associated with land-use change, water usage, and food security.

In conclusion, sustainable biofuel pathways hold immense potential for a greener future. The production of biofuels from organic matter offers a renewable and carbon-neutral alternative to conventional fossil fuels. By embracing biofuel technologies and policies, we can reduce our dependence on finite fossil fuel resources, mitigate climate change, and create a more sustainable and environmentally friendly energy sector. However, it is vital to carefully consider and address the potential challenges and impacts associated with biofuel production to ensure a truly sustainable and inclusive future for all.

Chapter 10: Conclusion

Summary of Key Findings

As we delve into the fascinating world of biofuels, it becomes evident that these alternative energy sources have the potential to shape the future of our world. In this subchapter, we aim to provide a concise yet comprehensive overview of the key findings presented throughout the book "Fueling the Future: Understanding Biofuel Policies and Regulations."

One of the primary findings in our exploration of biofuels is the immense potential they hold in reducing greenhouse gas emissions. Traditional fossil fuels have long been a major contributor to global warming and climate change. However, biofuels offer a renewable and sustainable alternative that can significantly mitigate these environmental concerns. Our research reveals that by replacing fossil fuels with biofuels, we can substantially reduce carbon dioxide emissions and work towards a greener, more sustainable future.

Furthermore, we have uncovered the importance of biofuel policies and regulations in fostering the growth and development of this industry. Governments around the world are recognizing the significance of biofuels in achieving their renewable energy targets. Our findings highlight the need for comprehensive and well-designed policies that provide incentives for biofuel production and consumption, while also addressing potential challenges such as land use competition and food security.

In our exploration, we have also examined the economic implications of biofuel adoption. Our research indicates that the biofuel industry has the potential to create new job opportunities and stimulate economic growth. However, we emphasize the importance of striking a balance between economic benefits and social considerations. It is crucial to ensure that biofuel production does not compromise food production or exacerbate poverty and inequality.

Additionally, our findings shed light on the importance of technological advancements and research in the biofuel sector. Innovations in biofuel production processes, such as cellulosic ethanol and algae-based biofuels, present promising solutions for increasing production efficiency and reducing costs. We highlight the need for continued investment in research and development to further enhance the viability of biofuels as a mainstream energy source.

In conclusion, our exploration of biofuel policies and regulations has revealed the significant potential of biofuels in addressing environmental, economic, and social challenges. As we move towards a more sustainable future, it is crucial for individuals, governments, and industries to understand the key findings presented in this book. By harnessing the power of biofuels, we can pave the way for a cleaner, greener, and more sustainable planet for generations to come.

Implications for Biofuel Industry and Stakeholders

In recent years, the biofuel industry has gained significant attention as an alternative to traditional fossil fuels. As concerns about climate change and the depletion of finite resources continue to grow, biofuels have emerged as a promising solution to mitigate these challenges. However, the implications of biofuel policies and regulations have far-reaching consequences for both the industry and its stakeholders.

One of the key implications for the biofuel industry is the need for sustainable feedstock production. Biofuels are produced from various organic materials, such as corn, sugarcane, and algae. As the demand for biofuels increases, it is crucial to ensure that feedstocks are produced in an environmentally and socially responsible manner. This entails implementing sustainable farming practices, minimizing water usage, and avoiding deforestation.

Moreover, biofuel policies and regulations have direct implications for the stakeholders involved in the industry. Farmers and agricultural communities stand to benefit from increased demand for biofuel feedstocks, as it provides them with additional revenue streams. However, it is vital to strike a balance to prevent the over-reliance on certain crops, which may lead to food shortages or price increases.

The transportation sector is another stakeholder affected by biofuel policies. With the implementation of biofuel blending mandates, fuel producers must incorporate a certain percentage of biofuels in their products. This not only reduces greenhouse gas emissions but also offers a more sustainable option for consumers. However, challenges arise in terms of infrastructure development and compatibility with existing engines. Investment in biofuel production and distribution infrastructure becomes essential to support the industry's growth.

Biofuel policies and regulations also have implications for the environment and climate change. By reducing carbon emissions, biofuels play a crucial role in mitigating climate change. However, the production of biofuels requires energy and resources, and if not managed properly, it can result in unintended environmental consequences. Striking a balance between biofuel production and environmental stewardship is essential for long-term sustainability.

In conclusion, the implications of biofuel policies and regulations are far-reaching, impacting various stakeholders and the environment. The biofuel industry must prioritize sustainability, ensuring responsible feedstock production and minimizing negative environmental impacts. Collaboration between policymakers, industry players, and communities is crucial to address the challenges and maximize the potential benefits of biofuel adoption. By understanding the implications, we can collectively work towards a future where biofuels play a significant role in achieving a sustainable and cleaner energy system.

Call to Action: Moving Towards a Sustainable Biofuel Future

In recent years, the world has witnessed an increasing interest in finding alternative sources of energy, and one of the most promising solutions lies in the development of biofuels. As concerns about climate change and the depletion of fossil fuels continue to grow, it is crucial for us all to come together and take action towards a sustainable biofuel future.

Biofuels, derived from organic matter such as plants and agricultural waste, offer a renewable and cleaner alternative to traditional fossil fuels. They have the potential to significantly reduce greenhouse gas emissions and mitigate the impact of climate change. Furthermore, biofuels can help decrease our dependence on imported oil and create new economic opportunities in the agricultural sector.

To achieve a sustainable biofuel future, it is essential to implement effective policies and regulations that promote the development and use of biofuels. Governments around the world must collaborate to create a supportive framework that incentivizes research, development, and investment in biofuel technologies. Additionally, there is a need for comprehensive legislation that ensures the sustainable production of feedstocks, such as crops and waste materials, to prevent negative environmental impacts.

However, the responsibility to move towards a sustainable biofuel future does not rest solely on the shoulders of policymakers. We all have a role to play in this transition. As consumers, we can make conscious choices by opting for biofuel-powered vehicles or supporting businesses that prioritize sustainability. By doing so, we create demand that will drive further innovation and investment in the biofuel industry.

Moreover, the agricultural sector can play a significant role in advancing biofuel production. Farmers can adopt sustainable practices that minimize the use of harmful inputs and promote the cultivation of biofuel feedstocks. By diversifying their crops and integrating bioenergy crops into their agricultural systems, farmers can contribute to both food security and the production of biofuels.

Education and awareness are also crucial in shaping a sustainable biofuel future. By spreading knowledge about the benefits of biofuels and their potential role in mitigating climate change, we can mobilize support and encourage individuals, businesses, and governments to take action.

In conclusion, the time to act is now. We must come together as a global community and move towards a sustainable biofuel future. By implementing supportive policies, making conscious choices as consumers, engaging the agricultural sector, and spreading awareness, we can create a greener and more sustainable world for future generations. Let us seize this opportunity and fuel the future with biofuels.

www.ingramcontent.com/pod-product-compliance
Lightning Source LLC
LaVergne TN
LVHW051955060526
838201LV00059B/3668